The Great Conspiracy - Part VI

JOHN ALEXANDER LOGAN

New York 1886

TABLE OF CONTENTS

FREEDOM'S SUN STILL RISING

After President Lincoln had issued his Proclamation of Emancipation, the friends of Freedom clearly perceived—and none of them more clearly than himself that until the incorporation of that great Act into the Constitution of the United States itself, there could be no real assurance of safety to the liberties of the emancipated; that unless this were done there would be left, even after the suppression of the Rebellion, a living spark of dissension which might at any time again be fanned into the flames of Civil War.

Hence, at all proper times, Mr. Lincoln favored and even urged Congressional action upon the subject. It was not, however, until the following year that definite action may be said to have commenced in Congress toward that end; and, as Congress was slow, he found it necessary to say in his third Annual Message: "while I remain in my present position I shall not attempt to retract or modify the Emancipation Proclamation; nor shall I return to Slavery any person who is Free by the terms of that Proclamation, or by any of the Acts of Congress,"

Meantime, however, occurred the series of glorious Union victories in the West, ending with the surrender to Grant's triumphant Forces on the 4th of July, 1863, of Vicksburg—"the Gibraltar of the West"—with its Garrison, Army, and enormous quantities of arms and munitions of war; thus closing a brilliant and successful Campaign with a blow which literally "broke the back" of the Rebellion; while, almost simultaneously, July 1-3, the Union Forces of the East, under Meade, gained the great victory of Gettysburg, and, driving the hosts of Lee from Pennsylvania, put a second and final end to Rebel invasion of Northern soil; gaining it, on ground dedicated by President Lincoln, before that year had closed—as a place of sepulture for the Patriot-soldiers who there had fallen in a brief, touching and immortal Address, which every American child should learn by heart, and every American adult ponder deeply, as embodying the very essence of true Republicanism.

[President Lincoln's Address, when the National Cemetery at Gettysburg, Pa., was dedicated Nov. 19, 1863, was in these memorable words:

"Fourscore and seven years ago, our Fathers brought forth upon this continent a new Nation, conceived in Liberty, and dedicated to the proposition that all men are created equal.

"Now we are engaged in a great Civil War, testing whether that Nation, or any Nation, so conceived and so dedicated, can long endure.

"We are met on a great battlefield of that War. We have come here to dedicate a portion of that field as a final resting-place for those who here gave their lives that that Nation might live.

"It is altogether fitting and proper that we should do this.

"But in a larger sense, we can not dedicate, we can not consecrate, we can not hallow, this ground. The brave men, living and dead, who struggled here, have consecrated it far above our power to add or detract.

"The World will little note, nor long remember, what we say here; but it can never forget what they did here.

"It is for us, the living, rather to be dedicated here to the unfinished work which they who fought here have, thus far, so nobly advanced.

"It is rather for us to be here dedicated to the great task remaining before us; that from these honored dead we take increased devotion to that Cause for which they gave the last full measure of devotion; that we here highly resolve that these dead shall not have died in vain; that this Nation, under God, shall have a new birth of Freedom; and that Government of the People, by the People, and for the People, shall not perish front the Earth."]

That season of victory for the Union arms, coming, as it did, upon a season of depression and doubtfulness, was doubly grateful to the loyal heart of the Nation. Daylight seemed to be breaking at last. Gettysburg had hurled back the Southern invader from our soil; and Vicksburg, with the immediately resulting surrender of Port Hudson, had opened the Mississippi river from Cairo to the Gulf, and split the Confederacy in twain. But it happened just about this time that, the enrollment of the whole Militia of the United States (under the Act of March, 1863), having been completed, and a Draft for 300,000 men ordered to be made and executed, if by a subsequent time the quotas of the various States should not be filled by volunteering, certain malcontents and Copperheads, inspired by agents and other friends of the Southern Conspirators, started and fomented, in the city of New York, a spirit of unreasoning opposition both to voluntary enlistment, and conscription under the Draft, that finally culminated, July

13th, in a terrible Riot, lasting several days, during which that great metropolis was in the hands, and completely at the mercy, of a brutal mob of Secession sympathizers, who made day and night hideous with their drunken bellowings, terrorized everybody even suspected of love for the Union, plundered and burned dwellings, including a Colored Orphan Asylum, and added to the crime of arson, that of murdering the mob-chased, terror-stricken Negroes, by hanging them to the lamp-posts.

These Riots constituted a part of that "Fire in the Rear" with which the Rebels and their Northern Democratic sympathizers had so frequently menaced the Armies of the Union.

Alluding to them, the N. Y. Tribune on July 15th, while its office was invested and threatened with attack and demolition, bravely said: "They are, in purpose and in essence, a Diversion in favor of Jefferson Davis and Lee. Listen to the yells of the mob and the harangues of its favorite orators, and you will find them surcharged with 'Nigger,' 'Abolition,' 'Black Republican,' denunciation of prominent Republicans, The Tribune, etc. etc.—all very wide of the Draft and the exemption. Had the Abolitionists, instead of the Slaveholders, revolted, and undertaken to upset the Government and dissolve the Union, nine-tenths of these rioters would have eagerly volunteered to put them down. It is the fear, stimulated by the recent and glorious triumphs of the Union Arms, that Slavery and the Rebellion must suffer, which is at the bottom of all this arson, devastation, robbery, and murder."

The Democratic Governor, Seymour, by promising to "have this Draft suspended and stopped," did something toward quieting the Riots, but it was not until the Army of the Potomac, now following Lee's retreat, was weakened by the sending of several regiments to New York that the Draft-rioting spirit, in that city, and to a less extent in other cities, was thoroughly cowed.

[In reply to Gov. Seymour's appeal for delay in the execution of the Draft Law, in order to test its Constitutionality, Mr. Lincoln, on the 7th of August, said he could not consent to lose the time that would be involved in obtaining a decision from the U. S. Supreme Court on that point, and proceeded: "We are contending with an Enemy who, as I understand, drives every able-bodied man he can reach into his ranks, very much as a butcher drives bullocks into a slaughter-pen. No time is wasted, no argument is used.

"This system produces an Army which will soon turn upon our now victorious soldiers already in the field, if they shall not be sustained by recruits as they should be.

It produces an Army with a rapidity not to be matched on our side, if we first waste time to re-experiment with the Volunteer system, already deemed by Congress, and palpably, in fact, so far exhausted as to be inadequate; and then more time to obtain a Court decision as to whether a law is Constitutional which requires a part of those not now in the Service to go to those who are already in it, and still more time to determine with absolute certainty that we get those who are to go, in the precisely legal proportion to those who are not to go.

"My purpose is to be in my action Just and Constitutional, and yet Practical, in performing the important duty with which I am charged, of maintaining the Unity and the Free principles of our common Country."]

Worried and weakened by this Democratic opposition to the Draft, and the threatened consequent delays and dangers to the success of the Union Cause, and depressed moreover by the defeat of the National forces under Rosecrans at Chickamauga; yet, the favorable determination of the Fall elections on the side of Union and Freedom, and the immense majorities upholding those issues, together with Grant's great victory (November, 1863) of Chattanooga—where the three days of fighting in the Chattanooga Valley and up among the clouds of Lookout Mountain and Mission Ridge, not only effaced the memory of Rosecrans's previous disaster, but brought fresh and imperishable laurels to the Union Arms—stiffened the President's backbone, and that of Union men everywhere.

Not that Mr. Lincoln had shown any signs of weakness or wavering, or any loss of hope in the ultimate result of this War for the preservation of the Union—which now also involved Freedom to all beneath its banner. On the contrary, a letter of his written late in August shows conclusively enough that he even then began to see clearly the coming final triumph— not perhaps as "speedy," as he would like, in its coming, but none the less sure to come in God's "own good time," and furthermore not appearing "to be so distant as it did" before Gettysburg, and especially Vicksburg, was won; for, said he: "The signs look better. The Father of Waters again goes unvexed to the Sea".

[This admirable letter, reviewing "the situation" and his policy, was in these words

EXECUTIVE MANSION,
WASHINGTON, August 26. 1863.
HON. JAMES C. CONKLING

MY DEAR SIR; Your letter inviting me to attend a Mass Meeting of unconditional Union men to be held at the Capital of Illinois, on the 3rd day of September, has been received. It would be very agreeable for me thus to meet my old friends at my own home; but I cannot just now be absent from here so long a time as a visit there would require.

The meeting is to be of all those who maintain unconditional devotion to the Union; and I am sure that my old political friends will thank me for tendering, as I do, the Nation's gratitude to those other noble men whom no partisan malice or partisan hope can make false to the Nation's life.

There are those who are dissatisfied with me. To such I would say: you desire Peace, and you blame me that we do not have it. But how can we attain it? There are but three conceivable ways: First, to suppress the Rebellion by force of Arms. This I am trying to do. Are you for it? If you are, so far we are agreed. If you are not for it, a second way is to give up the Union. I am against this. Are you for it? If you are, you should say so plainly. If you are not for Force, nor yet for Dissolution, there only remains some imaginable Compromise.

I do not believe that any Compromise embracing the maintenance of the Union is now possible. All that I learn leads to a directly opposite belief. The strength of the Rebellion is its Military, its Army. That Army dominates all the Country, and all the people, within its range. Any offer of terms made by any man or men within that range, in opposition to that Army, is simply nothing for the present: because such man or men have no power whatever to enforce their side of a Compromise, if one were made with them.

To illustrate: Suppose refugees from the South, and Peace men of the North, get together in Convention, and frame and proclaim a Compromise embracing a restoration of the Union. In what way can that Compromise be used to keep Lee's Army out of Pennsylvania? Meade's Army can keep Lee's Army out of Pennsylvania, and, I think, can ultimately drive it out of existence. But no paper Compromise to which the controllers of Lee's Army are not agreed, can at all affect that Army. In an effort at such Compromise we would waste time, which the Enemy would improve to our disadvantage; and that would be all.

A Compromise, to be effective, must be made either with those who control the Rebel Army, or with the people, first liberated from the domination of that Army, by the success of our own Army. Now, allow me to assure you that no word or intimation from that Rebel Army, or from any of the men controlling it, in relation to any Peace Compromise, has ever come to my knowledge or belief. All charges and insinuations to the contrary are deceptive and groundless. And I promise you that if any such proposition shall hereafter come, it shall not be rejected and kept a secret from you. I freely acknowledge myself to be the servant of the People, according to the bond of service, the United States Constitution; and that, as such, I am responsible to them.

But, to be plain. You are dissatisfied with me about the Negro. Quite likely there is a difference of opinion between you and myself upon that subject. I certainly wish that all men could be Free, while you, I suppose, do not. Yet I have neither adopted nor proposed any measure which is not consistent with even your view, provided that you are for the Union. I suggested compensated Emancipation; to which you replied you wished not to be taxed to buy Negroes. But I had not asked you to be taxed to buy Negroes, except in such a way as to save you from greater taxation to save the Union, exclusively by other means.

You dislike the Emancipation Proclamation, and perhaps would have it retracted. You say it is Unconstitutional. I think differently. I think the Constitution invests the Commander-in-Chief with the Law of War in Time of War. The most that can be said, if so much, is, that Slaves are property. Is there, has there ever been, any question that, by the Law of War, property, both of enemies and friends, may be taken when needed? And is it not needed whenever it helps us and hurts the Enemy? Armies, the World over, destroy enemies' property when they cannot use it; and even destroy their own to keep it from the Enemy. Civilized belligerents do all in their power to help themselves or hurt the Enemy, except a few things regarded as barbarous or cruel. Among the exceptions are the massacre of vanquished foes and non-combatants, male and female.

But the Proclamation, as law, either is valid or is not valid. If it is not valid, it needs no retraction. If it is valid it cannot be retracted, any more than the dead can be brought to life. Some of you profess to think its retraction would operate favorably for the Union. Why better after the retraction than before the issue? There was more than a year and a half of trial to suppress the Rebellion before the Proclamation was issued, the last one hundred days of which passed under an explicit notice that it was coming, unless averted by those in revolt returning to their allegiance. The War has certainly progressed as favorably for us since the issue of the Proclamation as before.

I know as fully as one can know the opinions of others that some of the Commanders of our Armies in the field, who have given us our most important victories, believe the Emancipation policy and the use of Colored troops constitute the heaviest blows yet dealt to the Rebellion, and that at least one of those important successes could not have been achieved when it was, but for the aid of Black soldiers.

Among the Commanders who hold these views are some who have never had an affinity with what is called "Abolitionism," or with "Republican party politics," but who hold them purely as Military opinions. I submit their opinions as entitled to some weight against the objections often urged that Emancipation and arming the Blacks are unwise as Military measures, and were not adopted as such, in good faith.

You say that you will not fight to Free Negroes. Some of them seem willing to fight for you; but no matter. Fight you, then, exclusively to save the Union. I issued the Proclamation on purpose to aid you in saving the Union. Whenever you shall have conquered all resistance to the Union, if I shall urge you to continue fighting, it will be an apt time then for you to declare you will not fight to Free Negroes. I thought that in your struggle for the Union, to whatever extent the Negroes should cease helping the

Enemy, to that extent it weakened the Enemy in his resistance to you. Do you think differently? I thought whatever Negroes can be got to do as soldiers, leaves just so much less for White soldiers to do in saving the Union. Does it appear otherwise to you? But Negroes, like other people, act upon motives. Why should they do anything for us if we will do nothing for them? If they stake their lives for us they must be prompted by the strongest motives, even the promise of Freedom. And the promise, being made, must be kept.

The signs look better. The Father of Waters again goes unvexed to the Sea. Thanks to the great Northwest for it; nor yet wholly to them. Three hundred miles up, they met New England, Empire, Keystone, and Jersey, hewing their way right and left. The Sunny South, too, in more colors than one, also lent a helping hand. On the spot, their part of the history was jotted down in Black and White. The job was a great National one, and let none be slighted who bore an honorable part in it. And while those who have cleared the Great River may well be proud, even that is not all. It is hard to say that anything has been more bravely and well done than at Antietam, Murfreesboro, Gettysburg, and on many fields of less note. Nor must Uncle Sam's web-feet be forgotten. At all the watery margins they have been present, not only on the deep Sea, the broad Bay, and the rapid River, but also up the narrow, muddy Bayou, and wherever the ground was a little damp they had been, and made their tracks. Thanks to all. For the Great Republic—for the principle it lives by, and keeps alive—for Man's vast future—thanks to all.

Peace does not appear so distant as it did. I hope it will come soon, and come to stay; and so come as to be worth the keeping in all future time. It will then have been proved that among Freemen there can be no successful appeal from the ballot to the bullet, and that they who take such appeal are sure to lose their case and pay the cost. And there will be some Black men who can remember that, with silent tongue, and clinched teeth, and steady eye, and well poised bayonet, they have helped mankind on to this great consummation, while I fear there will be some White ones unable to forget that with malignant heart and deceitful speech they have striven to hinder it. Still, let us not be over sanguine of a speedy, final triumph. Let us be quite sober. Let us diligently apply the means, never doubting that a just God, in his own good time, will give us the rightful result.

Yours very truly,

A. LINCOLN.]

But Chattanooga, and the grand majorities in all the Fall State-elections, save that of New Jersey,—and especially the manner in which loyal Ohio sat down upon the chief Copperhead-Democrat and Treason-breeder of the North, Vallandigham—came most auspiciously to strengthen the President's hands.

[The head of the Knights of the Golden Circle, and the Democratic candidate for Governor of Ohio]

And now he saw, more clearly still, the approach of that time when the solemn promise and declaration of Emancipation might be recorded upon the sacred roll of the Constitution, and thus be made safe for all time.

In his Annual Message of December, 1863, therefore, President Lincoln, after adverting to the fact that "a year ago the War had already lasted nearly twenty months," without much ground for hopefulness, proceeded to say:

"The preliminary Emancipation Proclamation, issued in September, was running its assigned period to the beginning of the New Year. A month later the final Proclamation came, including the announcement that Colored men of suitable condition would be received into the War service. The policy of Emancipation, and of employing Black soldiers, gave to the future a new aspect, about which hope, and fear, and doubt, contended in uncertain conflict.

"According to our political system, as a matter of Civil Administration, the General Government had no lawful power to effect Emancipation in any State, and for a long time it had been hoped that the Rebellion could be suppressed without resorting to it as a Military measure. It was all the while deemed possible that the necessity for it might come, and that if it should, the crisis of the contest would then be presented. It came, and, as was anticipated, it was followed by dark and doubtful days.

"Eleven months having now passed, we are permitted to take another view * * * Of those who were Slaves at the beginning of the Rebellion, full one hundred thousand are now in the United States Military service, about one half of which number actually bear arms in the ranks; thus giving the double advantage of taking so much labor from the Insurgent cause, and supplying the places which otherwise must be filled with so many White men. So far as tested, it is difficult to say they are not as good soldiers as any.

"No servile insurrection, or tendency to violence or cruelty, has marked the measures of Emancipation and arming the Blacks. These measures have been much discussed in Foreign Countries, and contemporary with such discussion the tone of public sentiment there is much improved. At home, the same measures have been fully discussed, supported, criticised, and denounced, and the annual elections following are highly encouraging to those whose official duty it is to bear the Country through this great trial. Thus we have the new reckoning. The crisis which threatened to divide the friends of the Union is past."

After alluding to his Proclamation of Amnesty, issued simultaneously with this Message, to all repentant Rebels who would take an oath therein prescribed, and contending that such an oath should be (as he had drawn it) to uphold not alone the Constitution and the Union, but the Laws and

Proclamations touching Slavery as well, President Lincoln continued:
"In my judgment they have aided and will further aid, the Cause for which they were intended. To now abandon them, would be not only to relinquish a lever of power, but would also be a cruel and an astounding breach of faith." And, toward the close of the Message, he added:
"The movements by State action, for Emancipation, in several of the States not included in the Emancipation Proclamation, are matters of profound gratulation. And while I do not repeat in detail what I have heretofore so earnestly urged upon the subject, my general views remain unchanged; and I trust that Congress will omit no fair opportunity of AIDING THESE IMPORTANT STEPS TO A GREAT CONSUMMATION."
Mr. Lincoln's patient but persistent solicitude, his earnest and unintermitted efforts—exercised publicly through his Messages and speeches, and privately upon Members of Congress who called upon, or whose presence was requested by him at the White House—in behalf of incorporating Emancipation in the Constitution, were now to give promise, at least, of bearing good fruit.
Measures looking to this end were submitted in both Houses of Congress soon after its meeting, and were referred to the respective Judiciary Committees of the same, and on the 10th of February, 1864, Mr. Trumbull reported to the Senate, from the Senate Judiciary Committee, of which he was Chairman, a substitute Joint Resolution providing for the submission to the States of an Amendment to the United States Constitution in the following words:
"ART. XIII., SEC. I. Neither Slavery nor Involuntary Servitude, except as a punishment for crime, whereof the party shall have been duly convicted, shall exist within the United States, or any place subject to their jurisdiction.
"SEC. II. Congress shall have power to enforce this Article by appropriate legislation."
This proposed Amendment came up for consideration in the Senate, on the 28th of March, and a notable debate ensued.
On the same day, in the House of Representatives, Thaddeus Stevens—with the object perhaps of ascertaining the strength, in that Body, of the friends of out-and-out Emancipation—offered a Resolution proposing to the States the following Amendments to the United States Constitution:
"ART. I. Slavery and Involuntary Servitude, except for the punishment of crimes whereof the party shall have been duly convicted, is forever prohibited in the United States and all its Territories.
"ART. II. So much of Article four, Section two, as refers to the delivery up of Persons held to Service or Labor, escaping into another State, is annulled."
The test was made upon a motion to table the Resolution, which motion was defeated by 38 yeas to 69 nays, and showed the necessity for converting

three members from the Opposition. Subsequently, at the instance of Mr. Stevens himself, the second Article of the Resolution was struck out by 72 yeas to 26 nays.

The proceedings in both Houses of Congress upon these propositions to engraft upon the National Constitution a provision guaranteeing Freedom to all men upon our soil, were now interrupted by the death of one who would almost have been willing to die twice over, if, by doing so, he could have hastened their adoption.

Owen Lovejoy, the life-long apostle of Abolitionism, the fervid gospeller of Emancipation, was dead; and it seemed almost the irony of Fate that, at such a time, when Emancipation most needed all its friends to make it secure, its doughtiest champion should fall.

But perhaps the eloquent tributes paid to his memory, in the Halls of Congress, helped the Cause no less. They at least brought back to the public mind the old and abhorrent tyrannies of the Southern Slave power; how it had sought not not only to destroy freedom of Action, but freedom of Speech, and hesitated not to destroy human Life with these; reminded the Loyal People of the Union of much that was hateful, from which they had escaped; and strengthened the purpose of Patriots to fix in the chief corner-stone of the Constitution, imperishable muniments of human Liberty.

Lovejoy's brother had been murdered at Alton, Illinois, while vindicating freedom of Speech and of the Press; and the blood of that martyr truly became "the seed of the Church." Arnold—recalling a speech of Owen Lovejoy's at Chicago, and a passage in it, descriptive of the martyrdom,— said to the House, on this sad occasion: "I remember that, after describing the scene of that death, in words—which stirred every heart, he said he went a pilgrim to his brother's grave, and, kneeling upon the sod beneath which sleeps that brother, he swore, by the everlasting God, eternal hostility to African Slavery." And, continued Arnold, "Well and nobly has he kept that oath."

Washburne, too, reminded the House of the memorable episode in that very Hall when, (April 5, 1860), the adherents of Slavery crowding around Lovejoy with fierce imprecations and threats, seeking then and there to prevent Free Speech, "he displayed that undaunted courage and matchless bearing which extorted the admiration of even his most deadly foes." "His"—continued the same speaker—"was the eloquence of Mirabeau, which in the Tiers Etat and in the National Assembly made to totter the throne of France; it was the eloquence of Danton, who made all France to tremble from his tempestuous utterances in the National Convention. Like those apostles of the French Revolution, his eloquence could stir from the lowest depths all the passions of Man; but unlike them, he was as good and as pure as he was eloquent and brave, a noble minded Christian man, a lover of the whole human Race, and of universal Liberty regulated by Law."

Grinnell, in his turn, told also with real pathos, of his having recently seen Lovejoy in the chamber of sickness. "When," said Grinnell, "I expressed fears for his recovery, I saw the tears course down his manly cheek, as he said 'Ah! God's will be done, but I have been laboring, voting, and praying for twenty years that I might see the great day of Freedom which is so near and which I hope God will let me live to rejoice in. I want a vote on my Bill for the destruction of Slavery, root and branch.'"

[Sumner, afterward speaking of Lovejoy and this Measure, said: "On the 14th of December, 1863, he introduced a Bill, whose title discloses its character: 'A Bill to give effect to the Declaration of Independence, and also to certain Provisions of the Constitution of the United States.' It proceeds to recite that All Men were Created Equal, and were Endowed by the Creator with the Inalienable Right to Life, Liberty and the Fruits of honest Toil; that the Government of the United States was Instituted to Secure those Rights; that the Constitution declares that No Person shall be Deprived of Liberty without due Process of Law, and also provides—article five, clause two—that this Constitution, and the Laws of the United States made in pursuance thereof, shall be the Supreme Law of the Land, and the Judges in each State shall be bound thereby, anything in the Constitution and Laws of any State to the contrary notwithstanding; that it is now demonstrated by the Rebellion that Slavery is absolutely incompatible with the Union, Peace, and General Welfare for which Congress is to Provide; and it therefore Enacts that All Persons heretofore held in Slavery in any of the States or Territories of the United States are declared Freedmen, and are Forever Released from Slavery or Involuntary Servitude except as Punishment for Crime on due conviction. On the same day he introduced another Bill to Protect Freedmen and to Punish any one for Enslaving them. These were among his last Public acts,"—Cong. Globe, 1st S., 38th C., Pt. 2, p. 1334]

And staunch old Thaddeus Stevens said: "The change to him, is great gain. The only regret we can feel is that he did not live to see the salvation of his Country; to see Peace and Union restored, and universal Emancipation given to his native land. But such are the ways of Providence. Moses was not permitted to enter the Promised Land with those he had led out of Bondage; he beheld it from afar off, and slept with his fathers." "The deceased," he impressively added, "needs no perishable monuments of brass or marble to perpetuate his name. So long as the English language shall be spoken or deciphered, so long as Liberty shall have a worshipper, his name will be known!"

What influence the death of Owen Lovejoy may have had on the subsequent proceedings touching Emancipation interrupted as we have seen by his demise—cannot be known; but among all the eloquent tributes to his memory called forth by the mournful incident, perhaps none, could he have heard it, would have better pleased him than those two opening sentences of Charles Summer's oration in the Senate—where he said of Owen Lovejoy: "Could his wishes prevail, he would prefer much that Senators should continue in their seats and help to enact into Law some one of the several Measures now pending to secure the obliteration of Slavery. Such an Act would be more acceptable to him than any personal tribute,—" unless it might be these other words, which followed from the same lips: "How his enfranchised Soul would be elevated even in those Abodes to which he has been removed, to know that his voice was still heard on Earth encouraging, exhorting, insisting that there should be no hesitation anywhere in striking at Slavery; that this unpardonable wrong, from which alone the Rebellion draws its wicked life, must be blasted by Presidential proclamation, blasted by Act of Congress, blasted by Constitutional prohibition, blasted in every possible way, by every available agency, and at every occurring opportunity, so that no trace of the outrage may continue in the institutions of the Land, and especially that its accursed foot-prints may no longer defile the National Statute-book. Sir, it will be in vain that you pass Resolutions in tribute to him, if you neglect that Cause for which he lived, and do not hearken to his voice!"

THIRTEENTH AMENDMENT IN THE SENATE

During the great debate, which now opened in the Senate, upon the Judiciary Committee's substitute resolution for the Amendment of the Constitution, so as forever to prohibit Slavery within the United States, and to empower Congress to pass such laws as would make that prohibition effective—participated in by Messrs. Trumbull, Wilson, Saulsbury, Davis, Harlan, Powell, Sherman, Clark, Hale, Hendricks, Henderson, Sumner, McDougall and others—the whole history of Slavery was enquired into and laid bare.

Trumbull insisted that Slavery was at the bottom of all the internal troubles with which the Nation had from its birth been afflicted, down to this wicked Rebellion, with all the resulting "distress, desolation, and death;" and that by 1860, it had grown to such power and arrogance that "its advocates demanded the control of the Nation in its interests, failing in which, they attempted its overthrow." He reviewed, at some length, what had been done by our Government with regard to Slavery, since the breaking out of hostilities against us in that mad attempt against the National life; how, "in the earlier stages of the War, there was an indisposition on the part of the Executive Authority to interfere with Slavery at all;" how, for a long time, Slaves, escaping to our lines, were driven back to their Rebel masters; how the Act of Congress of July, 1861, which gave Freedom to all Slaves allowed by their Rebel masters to assist in the erection of Rebel works and fortifications, had "not been executed," and, said Mr. Trumbull, "so far as I am advised, not a single Slave has been set at liberty under it;" how, "it was more than a year after its enactment before any considerable number of Persons of African descent were organized and armed" under the subsequent law of December, 1861, which not only gave Freedom to all Slaves entering our Military lines, or who, belonging to Rebel masters, were deserted by them, or were found in regions once occupied by Rebel forces and later by those of the Union, but also empowered the President to organize and arm them to aid in the suppression of the Rebellion; how, it was not until this law had been enacted that Union officers ceased to expel Slaves coming within our lines—and then only when dismissal from the public service was made the penalty for such expulsion; how, by his Proclamations of Emancipation, of September, 1862, and January, 1863, the President undertook to supplement Congressional action—which had, theretofore, been confined to freeing the Slaves of Rebels, and of such of these only as had come within the lines of our Military power-by also declaring, Free, the Slaves "who were in regions of country from which the authority of the United States was expelled;" and how, the "force and effect" of these Proclamations were variously understood by the enemies and friends of those measures—it being insisted on the one side that Emancipation as a War-stroke was within the Constitutional War-power of the President as Commander-in-Chief, and that, by virtue of those Proclamations, "all Slaves within the localities designated become ipso facto Free," and on the other, that the Proclamations were "issued without competent authority," and had not effected and could not effect, "the Emancipation of a single Slave," nor indeed could at any time, without additional legislation, go farther than to liberate Slaves coming within the Union Army lines.

After demonstrating that "any and all these laws and Proclamations, giving to each the largest effect claimed by its friends, are ineffectual to the destruction of Slavery," and protesting that some more effectual method of getting rid of that Institution must be adopted, he declared, as his judgment, that "the only effectual way of ridding the Country of Slavery, so that it cannot be resuscitated, is by an Amendment of the Constitution forever prohibiting it within the jurisdiction of the United States."

He then canvassed the chances of adoption of such an Amendment by an affirmative vote of two thirds in each House of Congress, and of its subsequent ratification by three-fourths of the States of the Union, and declared that "it is reasonable to suppose that if this proposed Amendment passes Congress, it will, within a year, receive the ratification of the requisite number of States to make it a part of the Constitution." His prediction proved correct—but only after a protracted struggle.

Henry Wilson also made a strong speech, but on different grounds. He held that the Emancipation Proclamations formed, together, a "complete, absolute, and final decree of Emancipation in Rebel States," and, being "born of Military necessity" and "proclaimed by the Commander-in-Chief of the Army and Navy, is the settled and irrepealable Law of the Republic, to be observed, obeyed, and enforced, by Army and Navy, and is the irreversible voice of the Nation."

He also reviewed what had been done since the outbreak of the Rebellion, by Congress and the President, by Laws and Proclamations; and, while standing by the Emancipation Proclamations, declared that "the crowning Act, in this series of Acts, for the restriction and extinction of Slavery in America, is this proposed Amendment to the Constitution prohibiting the existence of Slavery in the Republic of the United States."

The Emancipation Proclamation, according to his view, only needed enforcement, to give "Peace and Order, Freedom and Unity, to a now distracted Country;" but the "crowning act" of incorporating this Amendment into the Constitution would do even more than all this, in that it would "obliterate the last lingering vestiges of the Slave System; its chattelizing, degrading, and bloody codes; its malignant, barbarizing spirit; all it was, and is; everything connected with it or pertaining to it, from the face of the Nation it has scarred with moral desolation, from the bosom of the Country it has reddened with the blood and strewn with the graves of patriotism."

While the debate proceeded, President Lincoln watched it with careful interest. Other matters, however, had, since the Battle of Chattanooga, largely engrossed his attention.

The right man had at last been found—it was believed—to control as well as to lead our Armies. That man was Ulysses S. Grant. The grade of Lieutenant General of the Army of the United States—in desuetude since the days of Washington, except by brevet, in the case of Winfield Scott,—having been especially revived by Congress for and filled by the appointment and confirmation of Grant, March 2, 1864, that great soldier immediately came on to Washington, received his commission at the hands of President Lincoln, in the cabinet chamber of the White House, on the 9th, paid a flying visit to the Army of the Potomac, on the 10th, and at once returned to Nashville to plan future movements.

On the 12th, a General Order of the War Department (No. 98) was issued, relieving Major-General Halleck, "at his own request," from duty as "General-in-Chief" of the Army, and assigning Lieutenant-General U. S. Grant to "the command of the Armies of the United States," "the Headquarters of the Army" to be in Washington, and also with Lieutenant-General Grant in the Field, Halleck being assigned to "duty, in Washington, as Chief-of-staff of the Army, under the direction of the Secretary of War and the Lieutenant-General commanding."

By the same order, Sherman was assigned to the command of the "Military Division of the Mississippi," composed of the Departments of the Ohio, the Cumberland, the Tennessee, and the Arkansas; and McPherson to that of the Department and Army of the Tennessee.

On the 23rd of March, Grant was back again at Washington, and at once proceeded to Culpepper Court-house, Virginia, where his Headquarters in the field were, for a time, to be.

Here he completed his plans, and reorganized his Forces, for the coming conflicts, in the South-west and South-east, which were to result in a full triumph to the Union Arms, and Peace to a preserved Union.

It is evident, from the utterances of Mr. Lincoln when Vicksburg fell, that he had then become pretty well satisfied that Grant was "the coming man," to whom it would be safe to confide the management and chief leadership of our Armies. Chattanooga merely confirmed that belief—as indeed it did that of Union men generally. But the concurrent judgment of Congress and the President had now, as we have seen, placed Grant in that chief command; and the consequent relief to Mr. Lincoln, in thus having the heavy responsibility of Army-control, long unwillingly exercised by him, taken from his own shoulders and placed upon those of the one great soldier in whom he had learned to have implicit faith,—a faith earned by steady and unvaryingly successful achievements in the Field—must have been most grateful.

Other responsibilities would still press heavily enough upon the President's time and attention. Questions touching the Military and Civil government of regions of the Enemy's country, conquered by the Union arms; of the rehabilitation or reconstruction of the Rebel States; of a thousand and one other matters, of greater or lesser perplexity, growing out of these and other questions; besides the ever pressing and gigantic problems involved in the raising of enormous levies of troops, and prodigious sums of money, needed in securing, moving, and supplying them, and defraying the extraordinary expenses growing out of the necessary blockade of thousands of miles of Southern Coast, and other Naval movements; not to speak of those expenditures belonging to the more ordinary business transactions of the Government.

But chief of all things claiming his especial solicitude, as we have seen, was this question of Emancipation by Constitutional enactment, the debate upon which was now proceeding in the Senate. That solicitude was necessarily increased by the bitter opposition to it of Northern Copperheads, and by the attitude of the Border-State men, upon whose final action, the triumph or defeat of this great measure must ultimately depend.

Many of the latter, were, as has already been shown in these pages, loyal men; but the loyalty of some of these to their Country, was still so questionably and so thoroughly tainted with their worshipful devotion to Slavery—although they must have been blind indeed not to have discovered, long ere this, that it was a "slowly-dying cause"—that they were ever on the alert to delay, hamper, and defeat, any action, whether Executive or Legislative, and however necessary for the preservation of the Union and the overthrow of its mortal enemies, which, never so lightly, impinged upon their "sacred Institution."

This fact was well set forth, in this very debate, by a Senator from New England—[Wilson of Massachusetts]—when, after adjuring the anti-Slavery men of the age, not to forget the long list of Slavery's crimes, he eloquently proceeded:

"Let them remember, too, that hundreds of thousands of our countrymen in Loyal States—since Slavery raised the banners of Insurrection, and sent death, wounds, sickness, and sorrow, into the homes of the People—have resisted, and still continue to resist, any measure for the defense of the Nation, if that measure tended to impair the vital and animating powers of Slavery. They resisted the Act making Free the Slaves used by Rebels for Military purposes; the Confiscation of Rebel property and the Freedom of the Slaves of Rebel masters; the Abolition of Slavery in the Capital of the Nation, and the consecration of the Territories to Free Labor and Free laboring men; the Proclamation of Emancipation; the enlistment of Colored men to fight the battles of the Country; the Freedom of the Black soldier, who is fighting, bleeding, dying for the Country; and the Freedom of his wife and children. And now, when War has for nearly three years menaced the life of the Nation, bathed the Land in blood, and filled two hundred thousand graves with our slain sons, these men of the Loyal States still cling to the falling fortunes of the relentless and unappeasable Enemy of their Country and its democratic institutions; they mourn, and will not be comforted, over the expiring System, in the Border Slave-States; and, in tones of indignation or of anguish, they utter lamentations over the Proclamation of Emancipation, and the policy that is bringing Rebel States back again radiant with Freedom."

Among these "loyal" Democratic opponents of Emancipation, in any shape, or any where, were not wanting men—whether from Loyal Northern or Border States—who still openly avowed that Slavery was right; that Rebellion, to preserve its continuance, was justifiable; and that there was no Constitutional method of uprooting it.

Saulsbury of Delaware, was representative and spokesman of this class, and he took occasion during this very debate—[In the Senate, March 31, 1864.]—to defend Slavery as a Divine Institution, which had the sanction both of the Mosaic and Christian Dispensations!

[Said he: "Slavery had existed under some form or other from the first period of recorded history. It dates back even beyond the period of Abraham, the Father of the Faithful, in whose seed all the Nations of the Earth were to be blessed. We find that, immediately after the Flood, the Almighty, for purposes inscrutable to us, condemned a whole race to Servitude: 'Vayomer Orur Knoan Efet Afoatim Yeahio Le-echot:' 'And he said, Cursed be Canaan; Slave of Slaves he shall be to his brethren.' It continued among all people until the advent of the Christian era. It was recognized in that New Dispensation, which was to supersede the Old. It has the sanction of God's own Apostle; for when Paul sent back Onesimus to Philemon, whom did he send? A Freeman? No, Sir. He sent his (doulos,) a Slave, born as such, not even his andrapodon, who was such by captivity in War. Among all people, and in all ages, has this Institution, if such it is to be called, existed, and had the countenance of wise and good men, and even of the Christian Church itself, until these modern times, up at least to the Nineteenth Century. It exists in this Country, and has existed from the beginning."

Mr. Harlan's reply to the position of Mr. Saulsbury that Slavery is right, is a Divine Institution, etc., was very able and interesting. He piled up authority after authority, English as well as American, to show that there is no support of Slavery—and especially of the title to services of the adult offspring of a Slave—at Common Law; and, after also proving, by the mouth of a favorite son of Virginia, that it has no legal existence by virtue of any Municipal or Statutory Law, he declared that the only remaining Law that can be cited for its support is the Levitical Code"—as follows:

"'Both thy Bondmen, and thy Bondmaids, which thou shalt have, shall be of the heathen that are round about you; of them shall ye buy Bondmen and Bondmaids.

"'Moreover, of the children of the strangers that do sojourn among you, of them shall ye buy, and of their families that are with you, which they begat in your land; and they shall be your possession.

"'And ye shall take them as an Inheritance for your children after you, to inherit them for a possession; they shall be your Bondmen forever.'"

"I remark," said he, "in this connection, that the Levitical Code, or the Hebrew Law, contains a provision for the Naturalization of Foreigners, whether captives of War, or voluntary emigrants. By compliance with the requirements of this law they became citizens, entitled to all the rights and privileges and immunities of native Hebrews. The Hebrew Slave Code, applicable to Enslaved Hebrews, is in these words:

"'And if thy brother, an Hebrew man, or an Hebrew woman, be sold unto thee, and serve thee six years, then in the seventh year thou shalt let him go Free from thee.'

"Here I request the attention of those who claim compensation for Emancipated Slaves to the text:

"'And when thou sendest him out Free from thee, thou shalt not let him go away empty:

"'Thou shalt furnish him liberally out of thy floor'—

"Which means granaries—

"'and out of thy wine-press: of that wherewith the Lord thy God hath blessed thee, thou shalt give unto him.'

"'It shall not seem hard unto thee, when thou sendest him away Free from thee, for he hath been worth a double-hired servant to thee, in serving thee six years.'

"These Hebrew Statutes provide that the heathen might be purchased and held as Slaves, and their posterity after them; that under their Naturalization Laws all strangers and sojourners, Bond and Free, have the privilege of acquiring the rights of citizenship; that all Hebrews, natives or naturalized, might assert and maintain their right to Freedom.

"At the end of six years a Hebrew Slave thus demanding his Liberty, was not to be sent away empty; the owner, so far from claiming compensation from his neighbors or from the Public Treasury for setting him Free, was bound to divide with the Freedman, of his own possessions: to give him of his flocks, of his herds, of his granary, and of his winepress, of everything with which the Lord Almighty had blessed the master during the years of his Servitude; and then the owner was admonished that he was not to regard it as a hardship to be required to Liberate the Slave, and to divide with him of his substance.

"The Almighty places the Liberated Slave's claim to a division of his former master's property on the eternal principles of Justice, the duty to render an equivalent for an equivalent. The Slave having served six years must be paid for his Service, must be paid liberally because he had been worth even more than a hired servant during the period of his enslavement.

"If, then," continued Mr. Harlan, "the justice of this claim cannot be found either in Reason, Natural Justice, or the principles of the Common Law, or in any positive Municipal or Statute regulation of any State, or in the Hebrew Code written by the Finger of God protruded from the flame of fire on the summit of Sinai, I ask whence the origin of the title to the services of the adult offspring of the Slave mother? or is it not manifest that there is no just title? Is it not a mere usurpation without any known mode of justification, under any existing Code of Laws, human or Divine?"]

He also undertook to justify Secession on the singular ground that "we are sprung from a Race of Secessionists," the proof of which he held to be in the fact that, while the preamble to, as well as the body of the Convention of Ratification of, the old Articles of Confederation between the States of New Hampshire, Massachusetts Bay, Rhode Island and Providence Plantations, Connecticut, New York, New Jersey, Pennsylvania, Delaware, Maryland, Virginia, North Carolina, South Carolina, and Georgia, declared that Confederation to be a "Perpetual Union," yet, within nine years thereafter, all the other States Seceded from New York, Virginia, North Carolina, and Rhode Island by ratifying the new Constitution for "a more perfect Union."

He also endeavored to maintain the extraordinary proposition that "if the Senate of the United States were to adopt this Joint-resolution, and were to submit it to all the States of this Union, and if three-fourths of the States should ratify the Amendment, it would not be binding on any State whose interest was affected by it, if that State protested against it!" And beyond all this, he re-echoed the old, old cry of the Border-state men, that "the time is unpropitious for such a measure as this."

Reverdy Johnson, of Maryland, however, by his great speech, of April 5th, in the Senate, did much to clear the tangle in the minds of some faltering Union statesmen on this important subject.

He reviewed the question of human Slavery from the time when the Constitutional Convention was held; showed that at that period, as well as at the time of the Declaration of our Independence "there was but one sentiment upon the subject among enlightened Southern statesmen"—and that was, that Slavery "is a great affliction to any Country where it prevails;" and declared that "a prosperous and permanent Peace can never be secured if the Institution is permitted to survive."

He then traversed the various methods by which statesmen were seeking to prevent that survival of Slavery, addressing himself by turns to the arguments of those who, with John Sherman, "seemed," said he, "to consider it as within the power of Congress by virtue of its Legislative authority;" to those of the "many well-judging men, with the President at their head, who," to again use his own words, "seem to suppose that it is within the reach of the Executive;" and lastly, to those "who express the opinion that it is not within the scope of either Executive or Legislative authority, or of Constitutional Amendment;" and after demolishing the arguments of those who held the two former of these positions, he proceeded to rebut the assumption that Slavery could not be abolished at all because it was not originally abolished by the Constitution.

Continuing, he said: "Remember, now, the question is, can that Institution, which deals with Humanity as Property, which claims to shackle the mind, the soul, and the body, which brings to the level of the brute a portion of the race of Man, cease to be within the reach of the political power of the People of the United States, not because it was not at one time within their power, but because at that time they did not exert the power?

"What says the Preamble to the Constitution? How pregnant with a conclusive answer is the Preamble, to the proposition that Slavery cannot be abolished! What does that Preamble state to have been the chief objects that the great and wise and good men had at heart, in recommending the Constitution, with that Preamble, to the adoption of the American People? That Justice might be established; that Tranquillity might be preserved; that the common Defense and general Welfare might be maintained; and, last and chief of all, that Liberty might be secured.

"Is there no Justice in putting an end to human Slavery? Is there no danger to the Tranquillity of the Country in its existence? May it not interfere with the common Defense and general Welfare? And, above all, is it consistent with any notion, which the mind of man can conceive, of human Liberty?"

He held that the very Amendatory clause of the Constitution under which it was proposed to make this Amendment, was probably inserted there from a conviction of that coming time "when Justice would call so loudly for the extinction of the Institution that her call could not be disobeyed," and, when "the Peace and Tranquillity of the Land would demand, in thunder tones," its destruction, "as inconsistent with such Peace and Tranquillity."

To the atrocious pretence that "there was a right to make a Slave of any human being"—which he said would have shocked every one of the framers of the Constitution had they heard it; and, what he termed, the nauseous declaration that "Slavery of the Black race is of Divine origin," and was intended to be perpetual; he said:

"The Saviour of Mankind did not put an end to it by physical power, or by the declaration of any existing illegality, in word. His mission upon Earth was not to propagate His doctrines by force. He came to save, not to conquer. His purpose was not to march armed legions throughout the habitable Globe, securing the allegiance of those for whose safety He was striving. He warred by other influences. He aimed at the heart, principally. He inculcated his doctrines, more ennobling than any that the World, enlightened as it was before His advent upon Earth, had been able to discover. He taught to Man the obligation of brotherhood. He announced that the true duty of Man was to do to others as he would have others do to him—to all men, the World over; and unless some convert to the modern doctrine that Slavery itself finds not only a guarantee for its existence, but for its legal existence, in the Scripture, excepts from the operation of the influences which His morality brought to bear on the mind of the Christian world, the Black man, and shows that it was not intended to apply to Black men, then it is not true, it cannot be true, that He designed His doctrine not to be equally applicable to the Black and to the White, to the Race of Man as he then existed, or as he might exist in all after-time."

To the assumption that the African Slaves were too utterly deficient and degraded, mentally and morally, to appreciate the blessings of Freedom, he opposed the eloquent fact that "wherever the flag of the United States, the symbol of human Liberty, now goes; under it, from their hereditary bondage, are to be found men and women and children assembling and craving its protection 'fleeing from' the iron of oppression that had pierced their souls, to the protection of that flag where they are 'gladdened by the light of Liberty.'"

"It is idle to deny," said he—"we feel it in our own persons—how, with reference to that sentiment, all men are brethren. Look to the illustrations which the times now afford, how, in the illustration of that sentiment, do we differ from the Black man? He is willing to incur every personal danger which promises to result in throwing down his shackles, and making him tread the Earth, which God has created for all, as a man, and not as a

Slave."

Said he: "It is an instinct of the Soul. Tyranny may oppress it for ages and centuries; the pall of despotism may hang over it; but the sentiment is ever there; it kindles into a flame in the very furnace of affliction, and it avails itself of the first opportunity that offers, promising the least chance of escape, and wades through blood and slaughter to achieve it, and, whether it succeeds or fails, demonstrates, vindicates in the very effort, the inextinguishable right to Liberty."

He thought that mischiefs might result from this measure, owing to the uneducated condition of the Slave, but they would be but temporary. At all events to "suffer those Africans," said he, "whom we are calling around our standard, and asking to aid us in restoring the Constitution and the power of the Government to its rightful authority, to be reduced to bondage again," would be "a disgrace to the Nation." The "Institution" must be terminated.

"Terminate it," continued he, "and the wit of man will, as I think, be unable to devise any other topic upon which we can be involved in a fratricidal strife. God and nature, judging by the history of the past, intend us to be one. Our unity is written in the mountains and the rivers, in which we all have an interest. The very differences of climate render each important to the other, and alike important.

"That mighty horde which, from time to time, have gone from the Atlantic, imbued with all the principles of human Freedom which animated their fathers in running the perils of the mighty Deep and seeking Liberty here, are now there; and as they have said, they will continue to say, until time shall be no more: 'We mean that the Government in future shall be, as it has been in the past—Once an exemplar of human Freedom, for the light and example of the World; illustrating in the blessings and the happiness it confers, the truth of the principles incorporated into the Declaration of Independence, that Life and Liberty are Man's inalienable right."

Fortunately the Democratic opposition, in the Senate, to this measure, was too small in numbers to beat the proposed Amendment, but by offering amendments to it, its enemies succeeded in delaying its adoption.

However, on the 5th of April, an amendment, offered by Garrett Davis, was acted upon. It was to strike out all after the preamble of the XIIIth Article of Amendment to the Constitution, proposed by the Judiciary Committee, and insert the words:

"No Negro, or Person whose mother or grandmother is or was a Negro, shall be a citizen of the United States and be eligible to any Civil or Military office, or to any place of trust or profit under the United States."

Mr. Davis's amendment was rejected by a vote of 5 yeas to 32 nays; when he immediately moved to amend, by adding precisely the same words at the end of Section 1 of the proposed Article. It was again rejected. He then moved to amend by adding to the said Section these words:

"But no Slave shall be entitled to his or her Freedom under this Amendment if resident at the time it takes effect in any State, the laws of which forbid Free Negroes to reside therein, until removed from such State by the Government of the United States."

This also was rejected. Whereupon Mr. Powell moved to add, at the end of the first Section, the words:

"No Slave shall be Emancipated by this Article unless the owner thereof shall be first paid the value of the Slave or Slaves so Emancipated."

This likewise was rejected, on a yea and nay vote, by 2 yeas (Davis and Powell) to 34 nays; when Mr. Davis moved another amendment, viz.: to add at the end of Section 2 of the proposed Article, the following:

"And when this Amendment of the Constitution shall have taken effect by Freeing the Slaves, Congress shall provide for the distribution and settlement of all the population of African descent in the United States among the several States and Territories thereof, in proportion to the White population of each State and Territory to the aggregate population of those of African descent."

This met a like fate; whereupon the Senate adjourned, but, on the following day, the matter came up again for consideration:

Hale, of New Hampshire, jubilantly declared that "this is a day that I and many others have long wished for, long hoped for, long striven for. * * * A day when the Nation is to commence its real life; or, if it is not the day, it is the dawning of the day; the day is near at hand * * * when the American People are to wake up to the meaning of the sublime truths which their fathers uttered years ago, and which have slumbered, dead-letters, upon the pages of our Constitution, of our Declaration of Independence, and of our history."

McDougall, of California, on the other hand,—utterly regardless of the grandly patriotic resolutions of the Legislature of his State, which had just been presented to the Senate by his colleague—lugubriously declared:

"In my judgment, it may well be said of us:

'Let the Heavens be hung in black

And let the Earth put mourning on,'

for in the history of no Free People, since the time the Persians came down upon Athens, have I known as melancholy a period as this day and year of Our Lord in our history; and if we can, by the blessing of God and by His favor, rise above it, it will be by His special providence, and by no act of ours."

The obstructive tactics were now resumed, Mr. Powell leading off by a motion to amend, by adding to the Judiciary Committee's proposed Thirteenth Article of the Constitution, the following:

"ART. 14.—The President and Vice-President shall hold their Offices for the term of four—[Which he subsequently modified to: 'six years']—years. The person who has filled the Office of President shall not be reeligible."

This amendment was rejected by 12 yeas to 32 nays; whereupon Mr. Powell moved to add to the Committee's Proposition another new Article, as follows:

"ART. 14.—The principal Officer in each of the Executive Departments, and all persons connected with the Diplomatic Service, may be removed from office at the pleasure of the President. All other officers of the Executive Departments may be removed at any time by the President or other appointing power when their services are unnecessary, or for dishonesty, incapacity, inefficiency, misconduct, or neglect of duty, and when so removed, the removal shall be reported to the Senate, together with the reasons therefor."

This amendment also being rejected, Mr. Powell offered another, which was to add a separate Article as follows:

"ART. 14.—Every law, or Resolution having the force of law, shall relate to but one subject, and that shall be expressed in its title."

This also being rejected—the negative vote being, as in other cases, without reference to the merits of the proposition—and Mr. Powell having now apparently exhausted his obstructive amendatory talents, Mr. Davis came to the aid of his Kentucky colleague by moving an amendment, to come in as an additional Article, being a new plan of Presidential election designed to do away with the quadrennial Presidential campaign before the People by giving to each State the right to nominate one candidate, and leaving it to a Convention of both Houses of Congress—and, in case of disagreement, to the Supreme Court of the United States —to elect a President and a Vice-President.

The rejection of this proposition apparently exhausted the stock of possible amendments possessed by the Democratic opposition, and the Joint Resolution, precisely as it came from the Judiciary Committee, having been agreed to by that body, "as in Committee of the Whole," was now, April 6th, reported to the Senate for its concurrence.

On the following day, Mr. Hendricks uttered a lengthy jeremiad on the War, and its lamentable results; intimated that along the Mississippi, the Negroes, freed by the advance of our invading Armies and Navies, instead of being happy and industrious, were without protection or provision and almost without clothing, while at least 200,000 of them had prematurely perished, and that such was the fate reserved for the 4,000,000 Negroes if liberated; and declared he would not vote for the Resolution, "because," said he, "the times are not auspicious."

Very different indeed was the attitude of Mr. Henderson, of Missouri, Border-State man though he was. In the course of a speech, of much power, which he opened with an allusion to the 115,000 Slaves owned in his State in 1860—as showing how deeply interested Missouri "must be in the pending proposition"—the Senator announced that: "Our great interest, as lovers of the Union, is in the preservation and perpetuation of the Union." He declared himself a Slaveholder, yet none the less desired the adoption of this Thirteenth Article of Amendment, for, said he: "We cannot save the Institution if we would. We ought not if we could. * * * If it were a blessing, I, for one, would be defending it to the last. It is a curse, and not a blessing. Therefore let it go. * * * Let the iniquity be cast away!"

It was about this time that a remarkable letter written by Mr. Lincoln to a Kentuckian, on the subject of Emancipation, appeared in print. It is interesting as being not alone the President's own statement of his views, from the beginning, as to Slavery, and how he came to be "driven" to issue the Proclamation of Emancipation, and as showing how the Union Cause had gained by its issue, but also in disclosing, indirectly, how incessantly the subject was revolved in his own mind, and urged by him upon the minds of others. The publication of the letter, moreover, was not without its effect on the ultimate action of the Congress and the States in adopting the Thirteenth Amendment. It ran thus:

"EXECUTIVE MANSION.

"WASHINGTON, April 4, 1864.

"A. G. HODGES, Esq., Frankfort, Ky.

"MY DEAR SIR: You ask me to put in writing the substance of—what I verbally said the other day, in your presence, to Governor Bramlette and Senator Dixon. It was about as follows:

"I am naturally anti-Slavery. If Slavery is not wrong, nothing is wrong. I cannot remember when I did not so think and feel, and yet I have never understood that the 'Presidency conferred upon me an unrestricted right to act officially upon this judgment and feeling.

"It was in the oath I took, that I would to the best of my ability preserve, protect, and defend the Constitution of the United States. I could not take the Office without taking the oath. Nor was it my view that I might take an oath to get power, and break the oath in using the power.

"I understood, too, that in ordinary and Civil Administration this oath even forbade me to practically indulge my primary abstract judgment on the moral question of Slavery. I had publicly declared this many times, and in many ways.

"And I aver that, to this day, I have done no Official act in mere deference to my abstract judgment and feeling on Slavery.

"I did understand, however, that my oath to preserve the Constitution to the best of my ability, imposed upon me the duty of preserving by every indispensable means, that Government—that Nation, of which that Constitution was the Organic Law.

"Was it possible to lose the Nation and yet preserve the Constitution?

29

"By General Law, life and limb must be protected; yet often a limb must be amputated to save a life; but a life is never wisely given to save a limb. I felt that measures, otherwise Unconstitutional, might become lawful, by becoming Indispensable to the Constitution through the preservation of the Nation.

"Right or wrong, I assumed this ground, and now avow it. I could not feel that, to the best of my ability, I have even tried to preserve the Constitution, if, to save Slavery, or any minor matter, I should permit the wreck of Government, Country, and Constitution, altogether.

"When, early in the War, General Fremont attempted Military Emancipation, I forbade it, because I did not then think it an Indispensable Necessity.

"When, a little later, General Cameron, then Secretary of War, suggested the Arming of the Blacks, I objected, because I did not yet think it an Indispensable Necessity.

"When, still later, General Hunter attempted Military Emancipation, I again forbade it, because I did not yet think the Indispensable Necessity had come.

"When in March, and May, and July, 1862, I made earnest and successive appeals to the Border-States to favor compensated Emancipation, I believed the Indispensable Necessity for Military Emancipation and arming the Blacks would come, unless averted by that measure.

"They declined the proposition, and I was, in my best judgment, driven to the alternative of either surrendering the Union, and with it, the Constitution, or of laying strong hand upon the Colored element. I chose the latter. In choosing it, I hoped for greater gain than loss, but of this I was not entirely confident.

"More than a year of trial now shows no loss by it in our Foreign Relations, none in our home popular sentiment, none in our white Military force, no loss by it anyhow, or anywhere. On the contrary, it shows a gain of quite a hundred and thirty thousand soldiers, seamen, and laborers.

"These are palpable facts, about which, as facts, there can be no cavilling. We have the men; and we could not have had them without the measure.

"And now let any Union man who complains of this measure, test himself by writing down in one line, that he is for subduing the Rebellion by force of arms; and in the next, that he is for taking one hundred and thirty thousand men from the Union side, and placing them where they would be best for the measure he condemns. If he cannot face his case so stated, it is only because he cannot face the truth.

"I add a word which was not in the verbal conversation. In telling this tale, I attempt no compliment to my own sagacity. I claim not to have controlled events, but confess plainly that events have controlled me. Now at the end of three years' struggle, the Nation's condition is not what either Party, or any man, devised or expected. God alone can claim it.

"Whither it is tending seems plain. If God now wills the removal of a great wrong, and wills also that we of the North, as well as you of the South, shall pay fairly for our complicity in that wrong, impartial history will find therein new causes to attest and revere the Justice and goodness of God.

"Yours truly,

"A. LINCOLN."

The 8th of April (1864) turned out to be the decisive field-day in the Senate. Sumner endeavored to close the debate on that day in a speech remarkable no less for its power and eloquence of statement, its strength of Constitutional exposition, and its abounding evidences of extensive historical research and varied learning, than for its patriotic fervor and devotion to human Freedom.

Toward the end of that great speech, however, he somewhat weakened its force by suggesting a change in the phraseology of the proposed Thirteenth Amendment, so that, instead of almost precisely following the language of the Jeffersonian Ordinance of 1787, as recommended by the Judiciary Committee of the Senate, it should read thus:

"All Persons are Equal before the Law, so that no person can hold another as a Slave; and the Congress may make all laws necessary and proper to carry this Article into effect everywhere within the United States and the jurisdiction thereof."

Mr. Sumner's idea in antagonizing the Judiciary Committee's proposition with this, was to introduce into our Organic Act, distinctive words asserting the "Equality before the Law" of all persons, as expressed in the Constitutional Charters of Belgium, Italy and Greece, as well as in the various Constitutions of France—beginning with that of September, 1791, which declared (Art. 1) that "Men are born and continue Free and Equal in Rights;" continuing in that of June, 1793, which declares that "All Men are Equal by Nature and before the Law:" in that of June, 1814, which declares that "Frenchmen are Equal before the Law, whatever may be otherwise their title and ranks;" and in the Constitutional Charter of August, 1830 in similar terms to the last.

"But," said he, "while desirous of seeing the great rule of Freedom which we are about to ordain, embodied in a text which shall be like the precious casket to the more precious treasure, yet * * * I am consoled by the thought that the most homely text containing such a rule will be more beautiful far than any words of poetry or eloquence, and that it will endure to be read with gratitude when the rising dome of this Capitol, with the Statue of Liberty which surmounts it, has crumbled to dust."

Mr. Sumner's great speech, however, by no means ended the debate. It brought Mr. Powell to his feet with a long and elaborate contention against the general proposition, in the course of which he took occasion to sneer at

Sumner's "most remarkable effort," as one of his "long illogical rhapsodies on Slavery, like:
'—a Tale Told by an Idiot, full of sound and fury, Signifying nothing.'"
He professed that he wanted "the Union to be restored with the Constitution as it is;" that he verily believed the passage of this Amendment would be "the most effective Disunion measure that could be passed by Congress"—and, said he, "As a lover of the Union I oppose it."
[This phrase slightly altered, in words, but not in meaning, to "The Union as it was, and the Constitution as it is," afterward became the Shibboleth under which the Democratic Party in the Presidential Campaign of 1864, marched to defeat.]
He endeavored to impute the blame for the War, to the northern Abolitionists, for, said he: "Had there been no Abolitionists, North, there never would have been a Fire-eater, South,"—apparently ignoring the palpable fact that had there been no Slavery in the South, there could have been no "Abolitionists, North."
He heatedly denounced the "fanatical gentlemen" who desired the passage of this measure; declared they intended by its passage "to destroy the Institution of Slavery or to destroy the Union," and exclaimed: "Pass this Amendment and you make an impassable chasm, as if you were to put a lake of burning fire, between the adhering States and those who are out. You will then have to make it a War of conquest and extermination before you can ever bring them back under the flag of the Government. There is no doubt about that proposition."
Mr. Sumner, at this point, withdrew his proposed amendment, at the suggestion of Mr. Howard, who expressed a preference "to dismiss all reference to French Constitutions and French Codes, and go back to the good old Anglo-Saxon language employed by our Fathers, in the Ordinance of 1787, (in) an expression adjudicated upon repeatedly, which is perfectly well understood both by the public and by Judicial Tribunals—a phrase, which is peculiarly near and dear to the people of the Northwestern Territory, from whose soil Slavery was excluded by it."
[The following is the language of "the Ordinance of 1787" thus referred to:
"ART. 6.—There shall be neither Slavery nor Involuntary Servitude in the said Territory, otherwise than in the punishment of crimes, whereof the party shall have been duly convicted: * * *."]
Mr. Davis thereupon made another opposition speech and, at its conclusion, Mr. Saulsbury offered, as a substitute, an Article, comprising no less than twenty sections—that, he said, "embodied in them some things" which "did not meet his personal approbation," but he had consented to offer them to the Senate as "a Compromise"—as "a Peace offering."
The Saulsbury substitute being voted down, the debate closed with a speech by Mr. McDougall—an eloquent protest from his standpoint, in which,

after endorsing the wild statement of Mr. Hendricks that 250,000 of the people of African descent had been prematurely destroyed on the Mississippi, he continued.

"This policy will ingulf them. It is as simple a truth as has ever been taught by any history. The Slaves of ancient time were not the Slaves of a different Race. The Romans compelled the Gaul and the Celt, brought them to their own Country, and some of them became great poets, and some eloquent orators, and some accomplished wits, and they became citizens of the Republic of Greece, and of the Republic of Rome, and of the Empire.

"This is not the condition of these persons with whom we are now associated, and about whose affairs we undertake to establish administration. They can never commingle with us. It may not be within the reading of some learned Senators, and yet it belongs to demonstrated Science, that the African race and the European are different; and I here now say it as a fact established by science, that the eighth generation of the Mixed race formed by the union of the African and European, cannot continue their species. Quadroons have few children; with Octoroons reproduction is impossible.

"It establishes as a law of nature that the African has no proper relation to the European, Caucasian, blood. I would have them kindly treated. * * * Against all such policy and all such conduct I shall protest as a man, in the name of humanity, and of law, and of truth, and of religion."

The amendment made, as in Committee of the Whole, having been concurred in, etc., the Joint Resolution, as originally reported by the Judiciary Committee, was at last passed, (April 8th)—by a vote of 38 yeas to 6 nays—Messrs. Hendricks and McDougall having the unenviable distinction of being the only two Senators, (mis-)representing Free States, who voted against this definitive Charter of American Liberty.

[The full Senate vote, on passing the Thirteenth Amendment, was:

YEAS—Messrs. Anthony, Brown, Chandler, Clark, Collamer, Conness, Cowan, Dixon, Doolittle, Fessenden, Foot, Foster, Grimes, Hale, Harding, Harlan, Harris, Henderson, Howard, Howe, Johnson, Lane of Indiana, Lane of Kansas, Morgan, Morrill, Nesmith, Pomeroy, Ramsey, Sherman, Sprague, Sumner, Ten Eyck, Trumbull, Van Winkle, Wade, Wilkinson, Willey, and Wilson—38.

NAYs—Messrs. Davis, Hendricks, McDougall, Powell, Riddle, and Saulsbury.]

TREASON IN THE NORTHERN CAMPS

The immortal Charter of Freedom had, as we have seen, with comparative ease, after a ten days' debate, by the power of numbers, run the gauntlet of the Senate; but now it was to be subjected to the much more trying and doubtful ordeal of the House. What would be its fate there? This was a question which gave to Mr. Lincoln, and the other friends of Liberty and Union, great concern.

It is true that various votes had recently been taken in that body, upon propositions which had an indirect bearing upon the subject of Emancipation, as, for instance, that of the 1st of February, 1864, when, by a vote of 80 yeas to 46 nays, it had adopted a Resolution declaring "That a more vigorous policy to enlist, at an early day, and in larger numbers, in our Army, persons of African descent, would meet the approbation of the House;" and that vote, although indirect, being so very nearly a two-thirds vote, was most encouraging. But, on the other hand, a subsequent Resolution, squarely testing the sense of the House upon the subject, had been carried by much less than a two-thirds vote.

This latter Resolution, offered by Mr. Arnold, after conference with Mr. Lincoln, with the very purpose of making a test, was in these direct terms:

"Resolved, That the Constitution shall be so amended as to Abolish Slavery in the United States wherever it now exists, and to prohibit its existence in every part thereof forever."

The vote, adopting it, was but 78 yeas to 62 nays. * This vote, therefore, upon the Arnold Resolution, being nowhere near the two-thirds affirmative vote necessary to secure the passage through the House of the Senate Joint Resolution on this subject amendatory of the Constitution, was most discouraging.

It was definite enough, however, to show the necessity of a change from the negative to the affirmative side of at least fifteen votes. While therefore the outlook was discouraging it was far from hopeless. The debate in the Senate had already had its effect upon the public mind. That, and the utterances of Mr. Lincoln—and further discussion in the House, it was thought, might produce such a pressure from the loyal constituencies both in the Free and Border Slave-States as to compel success.

But from the very beginning of the year 1864, as if instinctively aware that their Rebel friends were approaching the crisis of their fate, and needed now all the help that their allies of the North could give them, the Anti-War Democrats, in Congress, and out, had been stirring themselves with unusual activity.

In both Houses of Congress, upon all possible occasions, they had been striving, as they still strove, with the venom of their widely-circulated speeches, to poison the loyal Northern and Border-State mind, in the hope that the renomination of Mr. Lincoln might be defeated, the chance for Democratic success at the coming Presidential election be thereby increased, and, if nothing else came of it, the Union Cause be weakened and the Rebel Cause correspondingly strengthened.

At the same time, evidently under secret instructions from their friends, the Conspirators in arms, they endeavored to create heart-burnings and jealousies and ill-feeling between the Eastern (especially the New England) States and the Western States, and unceasingly attacked the Protective-Tariff, Internal Revenue, the Greenback, the Draft, and every other measure or thing upon which the life of the Union depended.

Most of these Northern-Democratic agitators, "Stealing the livery of Heaven to serve the Devil in," endeavored to conceal their treacherous designs under a veneer of gushing lip-loyalty, but that disguise was "too thin" to deceive either their contemporaries or those who come after them. Some of their language too, as well as their blustering manner, strangely brought back to recollection the old days of Slavery when the plantation-whip was cracked in the House, and the air was blue with execration of New England.

Said Voorhees, of Indiana, (January 11, 1864) when the House was considering a Bill "to increase the Internal Revenue and for other purposes:"

"I want to know whether the West has any friends upon the floor of this House? We pay every dollar that is to be levied by this Tax Bill. * * * The Manufacturing Interest pays not a dollar into the public Treasury that stays there. And yet airs of patriotism are put on here by men representing that interest. I visited New England last Summer, * * * when I heard the swelling hum of her Manufactories, and saw those who only a short time ago worked but a few hands, now working their thousands, and rolling up their countless wealth, I felt that it was an unhealthy prosperity. To my mind it presented a wealth wrung from the labor, the sinews, the bone and muscle of the men who till the soil, taxed to an illegitimate extent to foster and support that great System of local wealth. * * * I do not intend to stand idly by and see one portion of the Country robbed and oppressed for the benefit of another."

And the same day, replying to Mr. Morrill of Vermont, he exclaimed: "Let him show me that the plethoric, bloated Manufacturers of New England are paying anything to support the Government, and I will recognize it."

Washburne, of Illinois got back at this part of Mr. Voorhees's speech rather neatly, by defending the North-west as being "not only willing to stand taxation" which had been "already imposed, but * * * any additional taxation which," said he, "may be necessary to crush out this Rebellion, and to hang the Rebels in the South, and the Rebel sympathizers in the North." And, he pointedly added: "Complaint has been made against New England. I know that kind of talk. I have heard too often that kind of slang about New England. I heard it here for ten years, when your Barksdales, and your Keitts's, and your other Traitors, now in arms against the Government, filled these Halls with their pestilential assaults not only upon New England, but on the Free North generally."

Kelley of Pennsylvania, however, more fitly characterized the speech of Voorhees, when he termed it "a pretty, indeed a somewhat striking, paraphrase of the argument of Mr. Lamar, the Rebel Agent,—[in 1886, Secretary of the Interior]—to his confreres in Treason, as we find it in the recently published correspondence: 'Drive gold coin out of the Country, and induce undue Importation of Foreign products so as to strike down the Financial System. You can have no further hope for Foreign recognition. It is evident the weight of arms is against us; and it is clear that we can only succeed by striking down the Financial System of the Country.' It was an admirable paraphrase of the Instructions of Mr. Lamar to the Rebel Agents in the North."

The impression was at this time abroad, and there were not wanting elements of proof, that certain members of Congress were trusted Lieutenants of the Arch-copperhead and Outlaw, Vallandigham. Certain it is, that many of these leaders, six months before, attended and addressed the great gathering from various parts of the Country, of nearly one hundred thousand Vallandigham-Anti-War Peace-Democrats, at Springfield, Illinois—the very home of Abraham Lincoln—which adopted, during a lull, when they were not yelling themselves hoarse for Vallandigham, a resolution declaring against "the further offensive prosecution of the War" as being subversive of the Constitution and Government, and proposing a National Peace Convention, and, as a consequence, Peace, "the Union as it was," and, substantially such Constitutional guarantees as the Rebels might choose to demand! And this too, at a time (June 13, 1863), when Grant, after many recent glorious victories, had been laying siege to Vicksburg, and its Rebel Army of 37,000 men, for nearly a month, with every reason to hope for its speedy fall.

No wonder that under such circumstances, the news of such a gathering of the Northern Democratic sympathizers with Treason, and of their adoption of such treasonable Resolutions, should encourage the Rebels in the same degree that Union men were disheartened! No wonder that Lee, elated by this and other evidences of Northern sympathy with Rebellion, at once determined to commence a second grand invasion of the North, and on the very next day (June 14th,) moved Northward with all his Rebel hosts to be welcomed, he fondly hoped, by his Northern friends of Maryland and elsewhere! As we have seen, it took the bloody Battle of Gettysburg to undeceive him as to the character of that welcome.

Further than this, Mr. Cox had stumped Ohio, in the succeeding election, in a desperate effort to make the banished Traitor, Vallandigham—the Chief Northern commander of the "Knights of the Golden Circle" (otherwise known as the "Order of the Sons of Liberty," and "O. A. K." or "Order of American Knights")—Governor of that great State.

[The Rebel General Sterling Price being the chief Southern commander of this many-named treasonable organization, which in the North alone numbered over 500,000 men.

August, 1864.—See Report of Judge Advocate Holt on certain "Secret Associations," in Appendix,]

And it only lacked a few months of the time when quantities of copies of the treasonable Ritual of the "Order of American Knights"—as well as correspondence touching the purchase of thousands of Garibaldi rifles for transportation to the West—were found in the offices of leading Democrats then in Congress.

When, therefore, it is said, and repeated, that there were not wanting elements of proof, outside of Congressional utterances and actions, that leading Democrats in Congress were trusted Lieutenants of the Supreme Commander of over half a million of Northern Rebel-sympathizers bound together, and to secrecy, by oaths, which were declared to be paramount to all other oaths, the violation of which subjected the offender to a shameful death somewhat like that, of being "hung, drawn, and quartered," which was inflicted in the middle ages for the crime of Treason to the Crown—it will be seen that the statement is supported by circumstantial, if not by positive and direct, evidence.

Whether the Coxes, the Garret Davises, the Saulsburys, the Fernando Woods, the Alexander Longs, the Allens, the Holmans, and many other prominent Congressmen of that sort,—were merely in close communion with these banded "Knights," or were actual members of their secret organizations, may be an open question. But it is very certain that if they all were not oath-bound members, they generally pursued the precise methods of those who were; and that, as a rule, while they often loudly proclaimed loyalty and love for the Union, they were always ready to act as if their loyalty and love were for the so-called Confederacy.

Indeed, it was one of these other "loyal" Democrats, who even preceded Voorhees, in raising the Sectional cry of: The West, against New England. It was on this same Internal Revenue Bill, that Holman of Indiana had, the day before Voorhees's attack, said:

"If the Manufacture of the Northwest is to be taxed so heavily, a corresponding rate of increase must be imposed on the Manufactures of New England and Pennsylvania, or, will gentlemen tax us without limit for the benefit of their own Section? * * * I protest against what I believe is intended to be a discrimination against one Section of the Country, by increasing the tax three-fold, without a corresponding increase upon the burdens of other Sections."

But these dreadfully "loyal" Democrats—who did the bidding of traitorous masters in their Treason to the Union, and thus, while posturing as "Patriots," "fired upon the rear" of our hard-pressed Armies—were super-sensitive on this point. And, when they could get hold of a quiet sort of a man, inclined to peaceful methods of discussion, how they would, terrier-like, pounce upon him, and extract from him, if they could, some sort of negative satisfaction!

Thus, for instance, on the 22nd of January, when one of these quiet men — Morris of New York—was in the midst of an inoffensive speech, Mr. Cox "bristled up," and blusteringly asked whether he meant to say that he (Cox) had "ever been the apologist or the defender of a Traitor?"

And Morris not having said so, mildly replied that he did "not so charge"— all of which little bit of by-play hugely pleased the touchy Mr. Cox, and his clansmen.

But on the day following, their smiles vanished under the words of Spalding or Ohio, who, after referring to the crocodile-tears shed by Democratic Congressmen over the Confiscation Resolution—on the pretense that it would hunt down "innocent women and children" of the Rebels, when they had never a word of sympathy for the widows and children of the two hundred thousand dead soldiers of the Union—continued:

"They can see our poor soldiers return, minus an arm, minus a leg, as they pass through these lobbies, but their only care is to protect the property of Rebels. And we are asked by one of my colleagues, (Mr. Cox) does the gentleman from New York intend to call us Traitors? My friend, Mr. Morris, modestly answered no! If he had asked that question of me, he knows what my answer would have been! I have seen Rebel officers at Johnson's Island, and I have taken them by the hand because they have fought us fairly in the field and did not seek to break down the Government while living under its protection. Yes, Sir, that gentleman knows that I would have said to him that I have more respect for an open and avowed Traitor in the field, than for a sympathizer in this Hall. Four months have scarcely gone by since that gentleman and his political friends were advocating the election of a man for the Gubernatorial office in my State, who was an open and avowed advocate of Secession—AN OUTLAW AT THAT!"

And old Thaddeus Stevens—the clear-sighted and courageous "Old Commoner"—followed up Spalding, and struck very close to the root and animus of the Democratic opposition, when he exclaimed:

"All this struggle by calm and dignified and moderate 'Patriots;' all this clamor against 'Radicals;' all this cry of 'the Union as it Was, and the Constitution as it Is;' is but a persistent effort to reestablish Slavery, and to rivet anew and forever the chains of Bondage on the limbs of Immortal beings. May the God of Justice thwart their designs and paralyze their wicked efforts!"

THE FIRE IN THE REAR

The treacherous purposes of professedly-loyal Copperheads being seen through, and promptly and emphatically denounced to the Country by Union statesmen, the Copperheads aforesaid concluded that the profuse circulation of their own Treason-breeding speeches—through the medium of the treasonable organizations before referred to, permeating the Northern States,—would more than counteract all that Union men could say or do. Besides, the fiat had gone forth, from their Rebel masters at Richmond, to Agitate the North.

Hence, day after day, Democrat after Democrat, in the one House or the other, continued to air his disloyal opinions, and to utter more or less virulent denunciations of the Government which guarded and protected him.

Thus, Brooks, of New York, on the 25th of January (1864), sneeringly exclaimed: "Why, what absurdity it is to talk at this Capitol of prosecuting the War by the liberation of Slaves, when from the dome of this building there can be heard at this hour the booming of cannon in the distance!"

Thus, also, on the day following, Fernando Wood—the same man who, while Mayor of New York at the outbreak of the Rebellion, had, under Rebel-guidance, proposed the Secession from the Union, and the Independence, of that great Metropolis,—declared to the House that: "No Government has pursued a foe with such unrelenting, vindictive malignity as we are now pursuing those who came into the Union with us, whose blood has been freely shed on every battle-field of the Country until now, with our own; who fought by our side in the American Revolution, and in the War of 1812 with Great Britain; who bore our banners bravest and highest in our victorious march from Vera Cruz to the City of Mexico, and who but yesterday sat in these Halls contributing toward the maintenance of our glorious institutions."

Then he went on, in the spirit of prophecy, to declare that: "No purely agricultural people, fighting for the protection of their own Domestic Institutions upon their own soil, have ever yet been conquered. I say further, that no revolted people have ever been subdued after they have been able to maintain an Independent government for three years." And then, warming up to an imperative mood, he made this explicit announcement: "We are at War. * * * Whether it be a Civil War, Rebellion, Revolution, or Foreign War, it matters little. IT MUST CEASE; and I want this Administration to tell the American People WHEN it will cease!" Again, only two days afterward, he took occasion to characterize a Bill, amendatory of the enrollment Act, as "this infamous, Unconstitutional conscription Act!"

C. A. White, of Ohio, was another of the malcontents who undertook, with others of the same Copperhead faith, to "maintain, that," as he expressed it, "the War in which we are at present engaged is wrong in itself; that the policy adopted by the Party in power for its prosecution is wrong; that the Union cannot be restored, or, if restored, maintained, by the exercise of the coercive power of the Government, by War; that the War is opposed to the restoration of the Union, destructive of the rights of the States and the liberties of the People. It ought, therefore, to be brought to a speedy and immediate close."

It was about this time also that, emboldened by immunity from punishment for these utterances in the interest of armed Rebels, Edgerton of Indiana, was put forward to offer resolutions "for Peace, upon the basis of a restoration of the Federal Union under the Constitution as it is," etc.

Thereafter, in both Senate and House, such speeches by Rebel-sympathizers, the aiders and abettors of Treason, grew more frequent and more virulent than ever. As was well said to the House, by one of the Union members from Ohio (Mr. Eckley):

"A stranger, if he listened to the debates here, would think himself in the Confederate Congress. I do not believe that if these Halls were occupied to-day by Davis, Toombs, Wigfall, Rhett, and Pryor, they could add anything to the violence of assault, the falsity of accusation, or the malignity of attack, with which the Government has been assailed, and the able, patriotic, and devoted men who are charged with its Administration have been maligned, in both ends of the Capitol. The closing scenes of the Thirty-Sixth Congress, the treasonable declarations there made, contain nothing that we cannot hear, in the freedom of debate, without going to Richmond or to the camps of Treason, where most of the actors in those scenes are now in arms against us."

With such a condition of things in Congress, it is not surprising that the Richmond Enquirer announced that the North was "distracted, exhausted, and impoverished," and would, "through the agency of a strong conservative element in the Free States," soon treat with the Rebels "on acceptable terms."

Things indeed had reached such a pass, in the House of Representatives especially, that it was felt they could not much longer go on in this manner; that an example must be made of some one or other of these Copperheads. But the very knowledge of the existence of such a feeling of just and patriotic irritation against the continued free utterance of such sentiments in the Halls of Congress, seemed only to make some of them still more defiant. And, when the 8th of April dawned, it was known among all the Democrats in Congress, that Alexander Long proposed that day to make a speech which would "go a bow-shot beyond them all" in uttered Treason. He would speak right out, what the other Conspirators thought and meant, but dared not utter, before the World.

A crowded floor, and packed galleries, were on hand to listen to the written, deliberate Treason, as it fell from his lips in the House. His speech began with an arraignment of the Government for treachery, incompetence, failure, tyranny, and all sorts of barbarous actions and harsh intentions, toward the Rebels—which led him to the indignant exclamation:

"Will they throw down their arms and submit to the terms? Who shall believe that the free, proud American blood, which courses with as quick pulsation through their veins as our own, will not be spilled to the last drop in resistance?"

Warming up, he proceeded to say: "Can the Union be restored by War? I answer most unhesitatingly and deliberately, No, never; 'War is final, eternal separation.'"

He claimed that the War was "wrong;" that it was waged "in violation of the Constitution," and would "if continued, result speedily in the destruction of the Government and the loss of Civil Liberty, and ought therefore, to immediately cease."

He held also "that the Confederate States are out of the Union, occupying the position of an Independent Power de facto; have been acknowledged as a belligerent both by Foreign Nations and our own Government; maintained their Declaration of Independence, for three years, by force of arms; and the War has cut asunder all the obligations that bound them under the Constitution."

"Much better," said he, "would it have been for us in the beginning, much better would it be for us now, to consent to a division of our magnificent Empire, and cultivate amicable relations with our estranged brethren, than to seek to hold them to us by the power of the sword. * * * I am reluctantly and despondingly forced to the conclusion that the Union is lost, never to be restored. * * * I see neither North nor South, any sentiment on which it is possible to build a Union. * * * in attempting to preserve our Jurisdiction over the Southern States we have lost our Constitutional Form of Government over the Northern. * * * The very idea upon which this War is founded, coercion of States, leads to despotism. * * * I now believe that there are but two alternatives, and they are either an acknowledgment of the Independence of the South as an independent Nation, or their complete subjugation and extermination as a People; and of these alternatives I prefer the former."

As Long took his seat, amid the congratulations of his Democratic friends, Garfield arose, and, to compliments upon the former's peculiar candor and honesty, added denunciation for his Treason. After drawing an effective parallel between Lord Fairfax and Robert E. Lee, both of whom had cast their lots unwillingly with the enemies of this Land, when the Wars of the Revolution and of the Rebellion respectively opened, Garfield proceeded:

"But now, when hundreds of thousands of brave souls have gone up to God under the shadow of the Flag, and when thousands more, maimed and shattered in the Contest, are sadly awaiting the deliverance of death; now, when three years of terrific warfare have raged over us, when our Armies have pushed the Rebellion back over mountains and rivers and crowded it back into narrow limits, until a wall of fire girds it; now, when the uplifted hand of a majestic People is about to let fall the lightning of its conquering power upon the Rebellion; now, in the quiet of this Hall, hatched in the lowest depths of a similar dark Treason, there rises a Benedict Arnold and proposes to surrender us all up, body and spirit, the Nation and the Flag, its genius and its honor, now and forever, to the accursed Traitors to our Country. And that proposition comes—God forgive and pity my beloved State!—it comes from a citizen of the honored and loyal Commonwealth of Ohio! I implore you, brethren in this House, not to believe that many such births ever gave pangs to my mother-State such as she suffered when that Traitor was born!"

As he uttered these sturdy words, the House and galleries were agitated with that peculiar rustling movement and low murmuring sound known as a "sensation," while the Republican side with difficulty restrained the applause they felt like giving, until he sadly proceeded:

"I beg you not to believe that on the soil of that State another such growth has ever deformed the face of Nature and darkened the light of God's day."

The hush that followed was broken by the suggestive whisper: "Vallandigham!"

"But, ah," continued the Speaker—as his voice grew sadder still—"I am reminded that there are other such. My zeal and love for Ohio have carried me too far. I retract. I remember that only a few days since, a political Convention met at the Capital of my State, and almost decided, to select from just such material, a representative for the Democratic Party in the coming contest; and today, what claims to be a majority of the Democracy of that State say that they have been cheated or they would have made that choice!"

[This refers to Horatio Seymour, the Democratic Governor of New York.]

After referring to the "insidious work" of the "Knights of the Golden Circle" in seeking "to corrupt the Army and destroy its efficiency;" the "riots and murders which," said he, "their agents are committing throughout the Loyal North, under the lead and guidance of the Party whose Representatives sit yonder across the aisle;" he continued: "and now, just as the time is coming on when we are to select a President for the next four years, one rises among them and fires the Beacon, throws up the blue-light—which will be seen, and rejoiced over, at the Rebel Capital in Richmond—as the signal that the Traitors in our camp are organized and ready for their hellish work! I believe the utterance of to-day is the uplifted banner of revolt. I ask you to mark the signal that blazes here, and see if there will not soon appear the answering signals of Traitors all over the Land. * * * If these men do mean to light the torch of War in all our homes; if they have resolved to begin the fearful work which will redden our streets, and this Capitol, with blood, the American People should know it at once, and prepare to meet it."

At the close of Mr. Garfield's patriotic and eloquent remarks, Mr. Long again got the floor, declared that what he had said, he believed to be right, and he would "stand by it," though he had to "stand solitary and alone," and "even if it were necessary to brave bayonets, and prisons, and all the tyranny which may be imposed by the whole power and force of the Administration."

Said he: "I have deliberately uttered my sentiments in that speech, and I will not retract one syllable of it." And, to "rub it in" a little stronger, he exclaimed, as he took his seat, just before adjournment: "Give me Liberty, even if confined to an Island of Greece, or a Canton of Switzerland, rather than an Empire and a Despotism as we have here to-day!"

This treasonable speech naturally created much excitement throughout the Country.

On the following day (Saturday, April 9, 1864), immediately after prayer, the reading of the Journal being dispensed with, the Speaker of the House (Colfax) came down from the Speaker's Chair, and, from the floor, offered a Preamble and Resolution, which ended thus:

"Resolved, That Alexander Long, a Representative from the second district of Ohio, having, on the 8th day of April, 1864, declared himself in favor of recognizing the Independence and Nationality of the so-called Confederacy now in arms against the Union, and thereby 'given aid, Countenance and encouragement to persons engaged in armed hostility to the United States,' is hereby expelled."

The debate which ensued consumed nearly a week, and every member of prominence, on both the Republican and Democratic sides, took part in it—the Democrats almost invariably being careful to protest their own loyalty, and yet attempting to justify the braver and more candid utterances of the accused member.

Mr. Cox led off, April 9th, in the defense, by counterattack. He quoted remarks made to the House (March 18, 1864) by Mr. Julian, of Indiana, to the effect that "Our Country, united and Free, must be saved, at whatever hazard or cost; and nothing, not even the Constitution, must be allowed to hold back the uplifted arm of the Government in blasting the power of the Rebels forever;"—and upon this, adopting the language of another—[Judge Thomas, of Massachusetts.]—Mr. Cox declared that "to make this a War, with the sword in one hand to defend the Constitution, and a hammer in the other to break it to pieces, is no less treasonable than Secession itself; and that, outside the pale of the Constitution, the whole struggle is revolutionary."

He thought, for such words as he had just quoted, Julian ought to have been expelled, if those of Long justified expulsion!

Finally, being pressed by Julian to define his own position, as between the Life of the Nation, and the Infraction of the United States Constitution, Mr. Cox said: "I will say this, that UNDER NO CIRCUMSTANCES CONCEIVABLE BY THE HUMAN MIND WOULD I EVER VIOLATE THAT CONSTITUTION FOR ANY PURPOSE!"

This sentiment was loudly applauded, and received with cries of "THAT IS IT!" "THAT'S IT!" by the Democratic side of the House, apparently in utter contempt for the express and emphatic declaration of Jefferson that: "A strict observance of the written laws is doubtless one of the highest duties of a good citizen, but it is not the highest. The laws of Necessity, of Self-preservation, of SAVING OUR COUNTRY WHEN IN DANGER, are of higher obligation. To LOSE OUR COUNTRY by a scrupulous adherence to written law WOULD BE TO LOSE THE LAW ITSELF, with Life, Liberty, Property, and all those who are enjoying them with us; thus absolutely SACRIFICING THE END TO THE MEANS."

[In a letter to J. B. Colvin, Sept. 20, 1810, quoted at the time for their information, and which may be found at page 542 of vol. v., of Jefferson's Works.]

Indeed these extreme sticklers for the letter of the Constitution, who would have sacrificed Country, kindred, friends, honesty, truth, and all ambitions on Earth and hopes for Heaven, rather than violate it—for that is what Mr. Cox's announcement and the Democratic endorsement of it meant, if they meant anything—were of the same stripe as those querulous Ancients, for the benefit of whom the Apostle wrote: "For THE LETTER KILLETH, but the Spirit giveth life."

And now, inspired apparently by the reckless utterances of Long, if not by the more cautious diatribe of Cox, Harris of Maryland, determining if possible to outdo them all, not only declared that he was willing to go with his friend Long wherever the House chose to send him, but added: "I am a peace man, a radical peace man; and I am for Peace by the recognition of the South, for the recognition of the Southern Confederacy; and I am for acquiescence in the doctrine of Secession." And, said he, in the midst of the laughter which followed the sensation his treasonable words occasioned, "Laugh as you may, you have got to come to it!" And then, with that singular obfuscation of ideas engendered, in the heads of their followers, by the astute Rebel-sympathizing leaders, he went on:

"I am for Peace, and I am for Union too. I am as good a Union man as any of you. [Laughter.] I am a better Union man than any of you! [Great Laughter.] * * * I look upon War as Disunion."

After declaring that, if the principle of the expulsion Resolution was to be carried out, his "friend," Mr. Long, "would be a martyr in a glorious cause"—he proceeded to announce his own candidacy for expulsion, in the following terms:

"Mr. Speaker, in the early part of this Secession movement, there was a Resolution offered, pledging men and money to carry on the War. My principles were then, and are now, against the War. I stood, solitary and alone, in voting against that Resolution, and whenever a similar proposition is brought here it will meet with my opposition. Not one dollar, nor one man, I swear, by the Eternal, will I vote for this infernal, this stupendous folly, more stupendous than ever disgraced any civilized People on the face of God's Earth. If that be Treason, make the most of it!

"The South asked you to let them go in peace. But no, you said you would bring them into subjugation. That is not done yet, and God Almighty grant that it never may be. I hope that you will never subjugate the South. If she is to be ever again in the Union, I hope it will be with her own consent; and I hope that that consent will be obtained by some other mode than by the sword. 'If this be Treason, make the most of it!'"

An extraordinary scene at once occurred—Mr. Tracy desiring "to know whether, in these Halls, the gentleman from Maryland invoked Almighty God that the American Arms should not prevail?" "Whether such language is not Treason?" and "whether it is in order to talk Treason in this Hall?"—his patriotic queries being almost drowned in the incessant cries of "Order!" "Order!" and great disorder, and confusion, on the Democratic side of the House.

Finally the treasonable language was taken down by the Clerk, and, while a Resolution for the expulsion of Mr. Harris was being written out, Mr. Fernando Wood—coming, as he said, from a bed of "severe sickness," quoted the language used by Mr. Long, to wit:

"I now believe there are but two alternatives, and they are either the acknowledgment of the Independence of the South as an independent Nation, or their complete subjugation and extermination as a People; and of these alternatives I prefer the former"—and declared that "if he is to be expelled for the utterance of that sentiment, you may include me in it, because I concur fully in that sentiment."

[He afterwards (April 11,) said he did not agree with Mr. Long's opinions.]

Every effort was unavailingly made by the Democrats, under the lead of Messrs. Cox—[In 1886 American Minister at Constantinople.]—and Pendleton,—[In 1886 American Minister at Berlin.]—to prevent action upon the new Resolution of expulsion, which was in these words:

"Whereas, Hon. Benjamin G. Harris, a member of the House of Representatives of the United States from the State of Maryland, has on this day used the following language, to wit: 'The South asked you to let them go in peace. But no; you said you would bring them into subjection. That is not done yet, and God Almighty grant that it never may be. I hope that you will never subjugate the South.' And whereas, such language is treasonable, and is a gross disrespect of this House: Therefore, Be it Resolved, That the said Benjamin G. Harris be expelled from this House."

Upon reaching a vote, however, the Resolution was lost, there being only 81 yeas, to 58 (Democratic) nays—two-thirds not having voted affirmatively. Subsequently, despite Democratic efforts to obstruct, a Resolution, declaring Harris to be "an unworthy Member" of the House, and "severely" censuring him, was adopted.

The debate upon the Long-expulsion Resolution now proceeded, and its mover, in view of the hopelessness of securing a two-thirds affirmative vote, having accepted an amendment comprising other two Resolutions and a Preamble, the question upon adopting these was submitted on the 14th of April. They were in the words following:

"Whereas, ALEXANDER LONG, a Representative from the second district of Ohio, by his open declarations in the National Capitol, and publications in the City of New York, has shown himself to be in favor of a recognition of the so-called Confederacy now trying to establish itself upon the ruins of our Country, thereby giving aid and comfort to the Enemy in that destructive purpose—aid to avowed Traitors, in creating an illegal Government within our borders, comfort to them by assurances of their success and affirmations of the justice of their Cause; and whereas, such conduct is at the same time evidence of disloyalty, and inconsistent with his oath of office, and his duty as a Member of this Body: Therefore,

"Resolved, That the said Alexander Long, a Representative from the second district of Ohio, be, and he is hereby declared to be an unworthy Member of the House of Representatives.

"Resolved, That the Speaker shall read these Resolutions to the said Alexander Long during the session of the House."

The first of these Resolutions was adopted, by 80 yeas to 69 nays; the second was tabled, by 71 yeas to 69 nays; and the Preamble was agreed to, by 78 yeas to 63 nays.

And, among the 63 Democrats, who were not only unwilling to declare Alexander Long "an unworthy Member," or to have the Speaker read such a declaration to him in a session of the House, but also refused by their votes even to intimate that his conduct evidenced disloyalty, or gave aid and comfort to the Enemy, were the names of such democrats as Cox, Eldridge, Holman, Kernan, Morrisson, Pendleton, Samuel J. Randall, Voorhees, and Fernando Wood.

Hence Mr. Long not only escaped expulsion for his treasonable utterances, but did not even receive the "severe censure" which, in addition to being declared (like himself) "an unworthy Member," had been voted to Mr. Harris for recklessly rushing into the breach to help him!

[The Northern Democracy comprised two well-recognized classes: The Anti-War (or Peace) Democrats, commonly called "Copperheads," who sympathized with the Rebellion, and opposed the War for the Union; and the War (or Union) Democrats, who favored a vigorous prosecution of the War for the preservation of the Union.]

THIRTEENTH AMENDMENT DEFEATED IN THE HOUSE

The debate in the House of Representatives, upon the Thirteenth Amendment to the Constitution—interrupted by the treasonable episode referred to in the last Chapter—was subsequently resumed.

Meanwhile, however, Fort Pillow had been stormed, and its garrison of Whites and Blacks, massacred.

And now commenced the beginning of the end—so far as the Military aspect of the Rebellion was concerned. Early in May, Sherman's Atlanta Campaign commenced, and, simultaneously, General Grant began his movement toward Richmond. In quick succession came the news of the bloody battles of the Wilderness, and those around Spottsylvania, Va.; at Buzzard Roost Gap, Snake Creek Gap, and Dalton, Ga.; Drury's Bluff, Va.; Resaca, Ga.; the battles of the North Anna, Va.; those around Dallas, and New Hope church, Ga; the crossing of Grant's forces to the South side of the James and the assault on Petersburg. While the Union Armies were thus valiantly attacking and beating those of the Rebels, on many a sanguinary field the loyal men of the North, both in and out of Congress, pressed for favorable action upon the Thirteenth Amendment. "Friends of the wounded in Fredericksburg from the Battle of the Wilderness"—exclaimed Horace Greeley in the New York Tribune, of May 31st,—"friends and relatives of the soldiers of Grant's Army beyond the Wilderness, let us all join hands and swear upon our Country's altar that we will never cease this War until African Slavery in the United States is dead forever, and forever buried!"

Peace Democrats, however, were deaf to all such entreaties. On the very same day, Mr. Holman, in the House, objected even to the second reading of the Joint Resolution Amendatory of the Constitution, and there were so many "Peace Democrats" to back him, that the vote was: 55 yeas to 76 nays, on the question "shall the Joint Resolution be rejected!"

The old cry, that had been repeated by Hendricks and others, in the Senate and House, time and again, was still used—threadbare though it was—"this is not the right time for it!" On this very day, for instance, Mr. Herrick said: "I ask if this is the proper time for our People to consider so grave a measure as the Amendment of the Constitution in so vital a point? * * * this is no fitting time for such work."

Very different was the attitude of Kellogg, of New York, and well did he show up the depths to which the Democracy—the Peace Democracy—had now fallen. "We are told," said he, "of a War Democracy, and such there are—their name is legion—good men and true; they are found in the Union ranks bearing arms in support of the Government and the Administration that wields it. At the ballot-box, whether at home or in the camp, they are Union men, and vote as they fight, and hold little in common with the political leaders of the Democratic Party in or out of this Hall—the Seymours, the Woods, the Vallandighams, the Woodwards, and their indorsers, who hold and control the Democratic Party here, and taint it with Treason, till it is a stench in the nostrils of all patriotic men."

After referring to the fact that the leaders of the Rebellion had from the start relied confidently upon assistance from the Northern Democracy, he proceeded:

"The Peace Democracy, and mere Party-hacks in the North, are fulfilling their masters' expectations industriously, unceasingly, and as far as in them lies. Not even the shouts for victory, in these Halls, can divert their Southern allies here. A sullen gloom at the defeat and discomfiture of their Southern brethren settles down on their disastrous countenances, from which no ray of joy can be reflected. * * * They even vote solid against a law to punish guerrillas.

"Sir," continued he, "in my judgment, many of those who withhold from their Country the support they would otherwise give, find allegiance to Party too strong for their patriotism. * * * Rejecting the example and counsels of Stanton and Dickinson and Butler and Douglas and Dix and Holt and Andrew Johnson and Logan and Rosecrans and Grant and a host of others, all Democrats of the straightest sect, to forget all other ties, and cleave only to their Country for their Country's sake, and rejecting the overtures and example of the Republican Party to drop and forget their Party name, that all might unite and band together for their Country's salvation as Union men, they turn a deaf ear and cold shoulder, and sullenly pass by on the other side, thanking God they are not as other men are, and lend, if at all, a calculating, qualified, and conditional and halting support, under protest, to their Country's cause; thus justifying the only hope of the

Rebellion to-day, that Party spirit at the North will distract its counsels, divide and discourage and palsy its efforts, and ultimately make way for the Traitor and the parricide to do their worst."

Besides the set speeches made against the proposed Constitutional amendment in the House, Peace-Democrats of the Senate continued to keep up a running fire at it in that Chamber, on every possible occasion. Garrett Davis was especially garrulous on the subject, and also launched the thunders of his wrath at the President quite frequently and even vindictively. For instance, speaking in the Senate—[May 31,1864,]—of the right of Property in Slaves; said he:

"This new-born heresy 'Military Necessity,' as President Lincoln claims, and exercises it, is the sum of all political and Military villianies * * * and it is no less absurd than it is villianous. * * * The man has never spoken or lived who can prove by any provision of the Constitution, or by any principle, or by any argument to be deduced logically and fairly from it, that he has any such power as this vast, gigantic, all-conquering and all-crushing power of Military Necessity which he has the audacity to claim.

"This modern Emperor, this Tiberius, a sort of a Tiberius, and his Sejanus, a sort of a Sejanus, the head of the War Department, are organizing daily their Military Courts to try civilians. * * *

"Sir, I want one labor of love before I die. I want the President of the United States, I want his Secretary of War, I want some of his high officers in Military command to bring a civilian to a Military execution, and me to have the proud privilege of prosecuting them for murder. * * * I want the law and its just retribution to be visited upon these great delinquents.

"I would sooner, if I had the power, bring about such an atonement as that, than I would even put down the Rebellion. It would be a greater victory in favor of Freedom and Constitutional Liberty, a thousand-fold, of all the People of America besides, than the subjugation of the Rebel States could possibly be."

But there seemed to be no end to the' attacks upon the Administration, made, in both Houses, by these peculiar Peace-Democrats. Union blood might flow in torrents on the fields of the rebellious South, atrocities innumerable might be committed by the Rebels, cold-blooded massacres of Blacks and Whites, as at Fort Pillow, might occur without rebuke from them; but let the Administration even dare to sneeze, and—woe to the Administration.

It was not the Thirteenth Amendment only, that they assailed, but everything else which the Administration thought might help it in its effort to put down the Rebellion. Nor was it so much their malignant activity in opposition to any one measure intended to strengthen the hands of the Union, but to all such measures; and superadded to this was the incessant bringing forward, in both Houses of Congress, by these restless Rebel-sympathizers, of Peace-Resolutions, the mere presentation of which would be, and were, construed by the Rebel authorities at Richmond, as evidences of a weakening.

Even some of the best of the Peace-Democrats, like S. S. Cox, for instance, not only assailed the Tariff—under which the Union Republican Party sought to protect and build up American Industry, as well as to raise as much revenue as possible to help meet the enormous current expenditures of the Government—but also denounced our great paper-money system, which alone enabled us to secure means to meet all deficiencies in the revenues otherwise obtained, and thus to ultimately conquer the hosts of Rebellion.

He declared (June 2, 1864) that "The People are the victims of the joint-robbery of a system of bounties under the guise of duties, and of an inconvertible and depreciated paper currency under the guise of money," and added: "No man is now so wise and gifted that he can save this Nation from bankruptcy. * * * No borrowing system can save us. The scheme of making greenbacks a legal tender, which enabled the debtor to cheat his creditor, thereby playing the old game of kingcraft, to debase the currency in order to aid the designs of despotism, may float us for a while amidst the fluctuations and bubbles of the day; but as no one possesses the power to repeal the Law of the Almighty, which decrees (and as our Constitution has established) that gold and silver shall be the standard of value in the World, so they will ever thus remain, notwithstanding the legislation of Congress."

Not satisfied with this sort of "fire in the rear," it was attempted by means of Democratic Free-Trade and antipaper-currency sophistries, to arouse jealousies, heart-burnings and resentful feelings in the breasts of those living in different parts of the Union—to implant bitter Sectional antagonisms and implacable resentments between the Eastern States, on the one hand, and the Western States, on the other—and thus, by dividing, to weaken the Loyal Union States.

That this was the cold-blooded purpose of all who pursued this course, would no doubt be warmly denied by some of them; but the fact remains no less clear, that the effect of that course, whether so intended or not, was to give aid and comfort to the Enemy at that critical time when the Nation most needed all the men, money, and moral as well as material support, it was possible to get, to put an end to the bloody Rebellion, now—under the continuous poundings of Grant's Army upon that of Lee in Virginia, and the advance of Sherman's Army upon that of Johnston in Georgia—tottering to its overthrow. Thus this same speaker (S. S. Cox), in his untimely speech, undertook to divide the Union-loving States "into two great classes: the Protected States and the Unprotected States;" and—having declared that "The Manufacturing States, mainly the New England States and Pennsylvania, are the Protected States," and "The Agricultural

States," mainly the eleven Western States, which he named, "are the Unprotected States"—proceeded to intemperately and violently arraign New England, and especially Massachusetts, in the same way that had years before been adopted by the old Conspirators of the South when they sought—alas, too successfully!—to inflame the minds of Southern citizens to a condition of unreasoning frenzy which made attempted Nullification and subsequent armed Rebellion and Secession possible.

Well might the thoroughly loyal Grinnell, of Iowa—after exposing what he termed the "sophistry of figures" by which Mr. Cox had seen fit "to misrepresent and traduce" the Western States—exclaim: "Sir, I have no words which I can use to execrate sufficiently such language, in arraying the Sections in opposition during a time of War; as if we were not one People, descended from one stock, having one interest, and bound up in one destiny!"

The damage that might have been done to the Union Cause by such malignant Democratic attacks upon the National unity and strength, may be imagined when we reflect that at this very time the annual expenses of our Government were over $600,000,000, and growing still larger; and that $1.90 in legal tender notes of the United States was worth but $1.00 in gold, with a downward tendency. Said stern old Thaddeus Stevens, alluding on this occasion, to Statesmanship of the peculiar stamp of the Coxes and Fernando Woods: "He who in this time will pursue such a course of argument for the mere sake of party, can never hope to be ranked among Statesmen; nay, Sir, he will not even rise to the dignity of a respectable Demagogue!"

Within a week after this, (June 9, 1864), we find in the Senate also, similarly insidious attacks upon the strength of the Government, made by certain Northern Democrats, who never tired of undermining Loyalty, and creating and spreading discontent among the People. The Bill then up, for consideration, was one "to prohibit the discharge of persons from liability to Military duty, by reason of the payment of money."

In the terribly bloody Campaign that had now been entered upon by Grant —in the West, under Sherman, and in the East, under his own personal eye—it was essential to send to the front, every man possible. Hence the necessity for a Bill of this sort, which moreover provided, in order as far as possible to popularize conscription, that all calls for drafts theretofore made under the Enrolling Act of March 3, 1863, should be for not over one year's service, etc.

This furnished the occasion for Mr. Hendricks, among other Peace Democrats, to make opposing speeches. He, it seems, had all along been opposed to drafting Union soldiers; and because, during the previous Winter, the Senate had been unwilling to abolish the clause permitting a drafted man to pay a commutation of $300 (with which money a substitute could be procured) instead of himself going, at a time when men were not quite so badly needed as now, therefore Mr. Hendricks pretended to think it very strange and unjustifiable that now, when everything depended on getting every possible man in the field, the Senate should think of "abandoning that which it thought right last Winter!"

He opposed drafting; but if drafting must be resorted to, then he thought that what he termed "the Horror of the Draft" should be felt by as many of the Union people as possible!—or, in his own words: "the Horror of the Draft ought to be divided among the People." As if this were not sufficient to conjure dreadful imaginings, he added: "if one set of men are drafted this year to serve twelve months, and they have to go because the power of the Government makes them go, whether they can go well or not, then at the end of the year their neighbors should be subjected to the same Horror, and let this dreadful demand upon the service, upon the blood, and upon the life of the People be distributed upon all."

And, in order apparently to still further intensify public feeling against all drafting, and sow the seeds of dissatisfaction in the hearts of those drafted at this critical time, when the fate of the Union and of Republican Government palpably depended upon conscription, he added: "It is not so right to say to twenty men in a neighborhood: 'You shall go; you shall leave your families whether you can or not; you shall go without the privilege of commutation whether you leave starving wives and children behind you or not,' and then say to every other man of the neighborhood: 'Because we have taken these twenty men for three years, you shall remain with your wives and children safely and comfortably at home for these three years.' I like this feature of the amendment, because it distributes the Horror of the Draft more equally and justly over the whole People."

Not satisfied with rolling the "Horror of the Draft" so often and trippingly over his tongue, he also essayed the role of Prophet in the interest of the tottering god of Slavery. "The People," said he, "expect great results from this Campaign; and when another year comes rolling around, and it is found that this War is not closed, and that there is no reasonable probability of its early close, my colleague (Lane) and other Senators who agree with him will find that the People will say that this effusion of blood must stop; that THERE MUST BE SOME ADJUSTMENT. I PROPHESY THIS."

And, as a further declaration likely to give aid and comfort to the Rebel leaders, he said: "I do not believe many men are going to be obtained by a draft; I do not believe a very good Army will be got by a draft; I do not believe an Army will be put in the field, by a draft, that will whip General Lee."

But while all such statements were, no doubt, intended to help the foes of the Union, and dishearten or dismay its friends, the really loyal People, understanding their fell object, paid little heed to them. The predictions of these Prophets of evil fell flat upon the ears of lovers of their Country. Conspirators, however much they might masquerade in the raiment of Loyalty, could not wholly conceal the ear-marks of Treason. The hand might be the hand of Esau, but the voice was the voice of Jacob.

On the 8th of June—after a month of terrific and bloody fighting between the immediate forces of Grant and Lee—a dispatch from Sherman, just received at Washington, was read to the House of Representatives, which said: "The Enemy is not in our immediate front, but his signals are seen at Lost Mountain, and Kenesaw." So, at the same time, at the National Capital, while the friends of the Union there, were not immediately confronted with an armed Enemy, yet the signals of his Allies could be seen, and their fire upon our rear could be heard, daily and almost hourly, both in the Senate and the House of Representatives.

The fight in the House, upon the Thirteenth Amendment, now seemed indeed, to be reaching a climax. During the whole of June 14th, until midnight, speech after speech on the subject, followed each other in rapid succession. Among the opposition speeches, perhaps those of Fernando Wood and Holman were most notable for extravagant and unreasoning denunciation of the Administration and Party in power—whose every effort was put forth, and strained at this very time to the utmost, to save the Union.

Holman, for instance, declared that, "Of all the measures of this disastrous Administration, each in its turn producing new calamities, this attempt to tamper with the Constitution threatens the most permanent injury." He enumerated the chief measures of the Administration during its three and a half years of power—among them the Emancipation Proclamation, the arming of the Blacks, and what he sneeringly termed "their pet system of finance" which was to "sustain the public credit for infinite years," but which "even now," said he, "totters to its fall!" And then, having succeeded in convincing himself of Republican failure, he exultingly exclaimed: "But why enumerate? What measure of this Administration has failed to be fatal! Every step in your progress has been a mistake. I use the mildest terms of censure!"

Fernando Wood, in his turn also, "mildly" remarked upon Republican policy as "the bloody and brutal policy of the Administration Party." He considered this "the crisis of the fate of the Union;" declared that Slavery was "the best possible condition to insure the happiness of the Negro race"—a position which, on the following day, he "reaffirmed"—and characterized those members of the Democratic Party who saw Treason in the ways and methods and expressions of Peace Democrats of his own stamp, as a "pack of political jackals known as War Democrats."

On the 15th of June, Farnsworth made a reply to Ross—who had claimed to be friendly to the Union soldier—in which the former handled the

Democratic Party without gloves. "What," said he, referring to Mr. Ross, "has been the course of that gentleman and his Party on this floor in regard to voting supplies to the Army? What has been their course in regard to raising money to pay the Army? His vote will be found recorded in almost every instance against the Appropriation Bills, against ways and means for raising money to pay the Army. It is only a week ago last Monday, that a Bill was introduced here to punish guerrillas * * * and how did my colleague vote? Against the Bill.* * * On the subject of arming Slaves, of putting Negroes into the Army, how has my colleague and his Party voted? Universally against it. They would strip from the backs of these Black soldiers, now in the service of the Country, their uniforms, and would send them back to Slavery with chains and manacles. And yet they are the friends of the soldier!"* * * "On the vote to repeal the Fugitive Slave Law, how did that (Democratic) side of the House vote? Does not the Fugitive Slave Law affect the Black soldier in the Army who was a Slave? That side of the House are in favor of continuing the Fugitive Slave Law, and of disbanding Colored troops. How did that side of the House vote on the question of arming Slaves and paying them as soldiers? They voted against it. They are in favor of disbanding the Colored regiments, and, armed with the Fugitive Slave Law, sending them back to their masters!"

He took occasion also to meet various Democratic arguments against the Resolution,—among them, one, hinging on the alleged right of Property in Slaves. This was a favorite idea with the Border-State men especially, that Slaves were Property—mere chattels as it were,—and, only the day before, a Northern man, Coffroth of Pennsylvania, had said:

"Sir, we should pause before proceeding any further in this Unconstitutional and censurable legislation. The mere abolition of Slavery is not my cause of complaint. I care not whether Slavery is retained or abolished by the people of the States in which it exists—the only rightful authority. The question to me is, has Congress a right to take from the people of the South their Property; or, in other words, having no pecuniary interest therein, are we justified in freeing the Slave-property of others? Can we Abolish Slavery in the Loyal State of Kentucky against her will? If this Resolution should pass, and be ratified by three-fourths of the States—States already Free—and Kentucky refuses to ratify it, upon what principle of right or law would we be justified in taking this Slave-property of the people of Kentucky? Would it be less than stealing?"

And Farnsworth met this idea—which had also been advanced by Messrs. Ross, Fernando Wood, and Pruyn—by saying: "What constitutes property? I know it is said by some gentlemen on the other side, that what the statute makes property, is property. I deny it. What 'vested right' has any man or State in Property in Man? We of the North hold property, not by virtue of statute law, not by virtue of enactments. Our property consists in lands, in chattels, in things. Our property was made property by Jehovah when He gave Man dominion over it. But nowhere did He give dominion of Man over Man. Our title extends back to the foundation of the World. That constitutes property. There is where we get our title. There is where we get our 'vested rights' to property."

Touching the ethics of Slavery, Mr. Arnold's speech on the same occasion was also able, and in parts eloquent, as where he said: 'Slavery is to-day an open enemy striking at the heart of the Republic. It is the soul and body, the spirit and motive of the Rebellion. It is Slavery which marshals yonder Rebel hosts, which confront the patriot Armies of Grant and Sherman. It is the savage spirit of this barbarous Institution which starves the Union prisoners at Richmond, which assassinates them at Fort Pillow, which murders the wounded on the field of battle, and which fills up the catalogue of wrong and outrage which mark the conduct of the Rebels during all this War.

"In view of all the long catalogue of wrongs which Slavery has inflicted upon the Country, I demand to-day, of the Congress of the United States, the death of African Slavery. We can have no permanent Peace, while Slavery lives. It now reels and staggers toward its last death-struggle. Let us strike the monster this last decisive blow."

And, after appealing to both Border-State men, and Democrats of the Free States, not to stay the passage of this Resolution which "will strike the Rebellion at the heart," he continued: "Gentlemen may flatter themselves with a restoration of the Slave-power in this Country. 'The Union as it was!' It is a dream, never again to be realized. The America of the past, has gone forever. A new Nation is to be born from the agony through which the People are now passing. This new Nation is to be wholly Free. Liberty, Equality before the Law, is to be the great Corner-stone."

So, too, Mr. Ingersoll eloquently said—among many other good things:—
"It is well to eradicate an evil. That Slavery is an evil, no sane, honest man will deny. It has been the great curse of this Country from its infancy to the present hour, And now that the States in Rebellion have given the Loyal States the opportunity to take off that curse, to wipe away the foul stain, I say let it be done. We owe it to ourselves; we owe it to posterity; we owe it to the Slaves themselves to exterminate Slavery forever by the adoption of the proposed Amendment to the Constitution. * * * I believe Slavery is the mother of this Rebellion, that this Rebellion can be attributed to no other cause but Slavery; from that it derived its life, and gathers its strength to-day. Destroy the mother, and the child dies. Destroy the cause, and the effect will disappear.

"Slavery has ever been the enemy of liberal principles. It has ever been the friend of ignorance, prejudice, and all the unlawful, savage, and detestable passions which proceed therefrom. It has ever been domineering, arrogant, exacting, and overbearing. It has claimed to be a polished aristocrat, when in reality it has only been a coarse, swaggering, and brutal boor. It has ever claimed to be a gentleman, when in reality it has ever been a villain. I think it is high time to clip its overgrown pretensions, strip it of its mask, and expose it, in all its hideous deformity, to the detestation of all honest and patriotic men."

After Mr. Samuel J. Randall had, at a somewhat later hour, pathetically and poetically invoked the House, in its collective unity, as a "Woodman," to "spare that tree" of the Constitution, and to "touch not a single bough," because, among other reasons, "in youth it sheltered" him; and furthermore, because "the time" was "most inopportune;" and, after Mr. Rollins, of Missouri, had made a speech, which he afterward suppressed; Mr. Pendleton closed the debate in an able effort, from his point of view, in which he objected to the passage of the Joint Resolution because "the time is not auspicious;" because, said he, "it is impossible that the Amendment proposed, should be ratified without a fraudulent use of the power to admit new States, or a fraudulent use of the Military power of the Federal Government in the Seceded States,"—and, said he, "if you should attempt to amend the Constitution by such means, what binding obligation would it have?"

He objected, also, because "the States cannot, under the pretense of amending the Constitution, subvert the structure, spirit, and theory of this Government." "But," said he, "if this Amendment were within the Constitutional power of amendment; if this were a proper time to consider it; if three-fourths of the States were willing to ratify it; and if it did not require the fraudulent use of power, either in this House or in the Executive Department, to secure its adoption, I would still resist the passage of this Resolution. It is another step toward consolidation, and consolidation is Despotism; confederation is Liberty."

It was about 4 o'clock in the afternoon of June 15th, that the House came to a vote, on the passage of the Joint Resolution. At first the strain of anxiety on both sides was great, but, as the roll proceeded, it soon became evident that the Resolution was doomed to defeat. And so it transpired. The vote stood 93 yeas, to 65 nays—Mr. Ashley having changed his vote, from the affirmative to the negative, for the purpose of submitting, at the proper time, a motion to reconsider.

That same evening, Mr. Ashley made the motion to reconsider the vote by which the proposed Constitutional Amendment was rejected; and the motion was duly entered in the Journal, despite the persistent efforts of Messrs. Cox, Holman, and others, to prevent it.

On the 28th of June, just prior to the Congressional Recess, Mr. Ashley announced that he had been disappointed in the hope of securing enough votes from the Democratic side of the House to carry the Amendment.

"Those," said he, "who ought to have been the champions of this great proposition are unfortunately its strongest opponents. They have permitted the golden opportunity to pass. The record is made up, and we must go to the Country on this issue thus presented." And then he gave notice that he would call the matter up, at the earliest possible moment after the opening of the December Session of Congress.

SLAVERY DOOMED AT THE POLLS

The record was indeed made up, and the issue thus made, between Slavery and Freedom, would be the chief one before the People. Already the Republican National Convention, which met at Baltimore, June 7, 1864, had not only with "enthusiastic unanimity," renominated Mr. Lincoln for the Presidency, but amid "tremendous applause," the delegates rising and waving their hats—had adopted a platform which declared, in behalf of that great Party: "That, as Slavery was the cause, and now constitutes the strength, of this Rebellion, and as it must be, always and everywhere, hostile to the principles of Republican government, Justice and the National safety demand its utter and complete extirpation from the soil of the Republic; and that while we uphold and maintain the Acts and Proclamations by which the Government, in its own defense, has aimed a death-blow at this gigantic evil, we are in favor, furthermore, of such an Amendment to the Constitution, to be made by the People in conformity with its provisions, as shall terminate and forever prohibit the existence of Slavery within the limits or the jurisdiction of the United States."

So, too, with vociferous plaudits, had they received and adopted another Resolution, wherein they declared "That we approve and applaud the practical wisdom, the unselfish patriotism and the unswerving fidelity to the Constitution and the principles of American Liberty, with which Abraham Lincoln has discharged, under circumstances of unparalleled difficulty, the great duties and responsibilities of the Presidential Office; that we approve and endorse, as demanded by the emergency, and essential to the preservation of the Nation, and as within the provisions of the Constitution; the Measures and Acts which he has adopted to defend the Nation against its open and secret foes; that we approve, especially, the Proclamation of Emancipation, and the employment, as Union soldiers, of men heretofore held in Slavery; and that we have full confidence in his determination to carry these and all other Constitutional Measures essential to the salvation of the Country, into full and complete effect."

Thus heartily, thoroughly and unreservedly, endorsed in all the great acts of his Administration—and even more emphatically, if possible, in his Emancipation policy—by the unanimous vote of his Party, Mr. Lincoln, although necessarily "chagrined and disappointed" by the House-vote which had defeated the Thirteenth Amendment, might well feel undismayed. He always had implicit faith in the People; he felt sure that they would sustain him; and this done, why could not the votes of a dozen, out of the seventy Congressional Representatives opposing that Amendment, be changed? Even failing in this, it must be but a question of time. He thought he could afford to bide that time.

On the 29th of August, the Democratic National Convention met at Chicago. Horatio Seymour was its permanent President; that same Governor of New York whom the 4th of July, 1863, almost at the moment when Vicksburg and Gettysburg had brought great encouragement to the Union cause, and when public necessity demanded the enforcement of the Draft in order to drive the Rebel invader from Northern soil and bring the Rebellion speedily to an end—had threateningly said to the Republicans, in the course of a public speech, during the Draft-riots at New York City: "Remember this, that the bloody, and treasonable, and revolutionary doctrine of public necessity can be proclaimed by a mob as well as by a Government. * * * When men accept despotism, they may have a choice as to who the despot shall be!"

In his speech to this Democratic-Copperhead National Convention, therefore, it is not surprising that he should, at this time, declare that "this Administration cannot now save this Union, if it would." That the body which elected such a presiding officer,—after the bloody series of glorious Union victories about Atlanta, Ga., then fast leading up to the fall of that great Rebel stronghold, (which event actually occurred long before most of these Democratic delegates, on their return, could even reach their homes)—should adopt a Resolution declaring that the War was a "failure," was not surprising either.

That Resolution—"the material resolution of the Chicago platform," as Vallandigham afterward characters it, was written and "carried through both the Subcommittee and the General Committee" by that Arch-Copperhead and Conspirator himself.—[See his letter of October 22, 1864, to the editor of the New York News,]

It was in these words: "Resolved, That this Convention does explicitly declare as the sense of the American People, that after four years of failure to restore the Union by the experiment of War, during which, under the pretense of a military necessity, or War—power higher than the

Constitution, the Constitution itself has been disregarded in every part, and public Liberty and private right alike trodden down and the material prosperity of the Country essentially impaired—Justice, Humanity, Liberty, and the public welfare demand that immediate efforts be made for a cessation of hostilities, with a view to an ultimate Convention of the States, or other peaceable means, to the end that at the earliest practicable moment Peace may be restored on the basis of the Federal Union of the States."

With a Copperhead platform, this Democratic Convention thought it politic to have a Union candidate for the Presidency. Hence, the nomination of General McClellan; but to propitiate the out-and-out Vallandigham Peace men, Mr. Pendleton was nominated to the second place on the ticket.

This combination was almost as great a blunder as was the platform—than which nothing could have been worse. Farragut's Naval victory at Mobile, and Sherman's capture of Atlanta, followed so closely upon the adjournment of the Convention as to make its platform and candidates the laughing stock of the Nation; and all the efforts of Democratic orators, and of McClellan himself, in his letter of acceptance, could not prevent the rise of that great tidal wave of Unionism which was soon to engulf the hosts of Copperhead-Democracy.

The Thanksgiving-services in the churches, and the thundering salutes of 100 guns from every Military and Naval post in the United States, which — during the week succeeding that Convention's sitting—betokened the Nation's especial joy and gratitude to the victorious Union Forces of Sherman and Farragut for their fortuitously-timed demonstration that the "experiment of War" for the restoration of the Union was anything but a "Failure" all helped to add to the proportions of that rapidly-swelling volume of loyal public feeling.

The withdrawal from the canvass, of General Fremont, nominated for the Presidency by the "radical men of the Nation," at Cleveland, also contributed to it. In his letter of withdrawal, September 17th, he said:

"The Presidential contest has, in effect, been entered upon in such a way that the union of the Republican Party has become a paramount necessity. The policy of the Democratic Party signifies either separation, or reestablishment with Slavery. The Chicago platform is simply separation. General McClellan's letter of acceptance is reestablishment, with Slavery. The Republican candidate is, on the contrary, pledged to the reestablishment of the Union without Slavery; and, however hesitating his policy may be, the pressure of his Party will, we may hope, force him to it. Between these issues, I think no man of the Liberal Party can remain in doubt."

And now, following the fall of Atlanta before Sherman's Forces, Grant had stormed "Fort Hell," in front of Petersburg; Sheridan had routed the Rebels, under Early, at Winchester, and had again defeated Early at Fisher's

Hill; Lee had been repulsed in his attack on Grant's works at Petersburg; and Allatoona had been made famous, by Corse and his 2,000 Union men gallantly repulsing the 5,000 men of Hood's Rebel Army, who had completely surrounded and attacked them in front, flank, and rear.

All these Military successes for the Union Cause helped the Union political campaign considerably, and, when supplemented by the remarkable results of the October elections in Pennsylvania, Indiana, and Maryland, made the election of Lincoln and Johnson a foregone conclusion.

The sudden death of Chief-Justice Taney, too, happening, by a strange coincidence, simultaneously with the triumph of the Union Party of Maryland in carrying the new Constitution of that State, which prohibited Slavery within her borders, seemed to have a significance* not without its effect upon the public mind, now fast settling down to the belief that Slavery everywhere upon the soil of the United States must die.

[Greeley well said of it: "His death, at this moment, seemed to mark the transition from the Era of Slavery to that of Universal Freedom."]

Then came, October 19th, the Battle of Cedar Creek, Va. where the Rebel General Early, during Sheridan's absence, surprised and defeated the latter's forces, until Sheridan, riding down from Winchester, turned defeat into victory for the Union Arms, and chased the armed Rebels out of the Shenandoah Valley forever; and the fights of October 27th and 28th, to the left of Grant's position, at Petersburg, by which the railroad communications of Lee's Army at Richmond were broken up.

At last, November 8, 1864, dawned the eventful day of election. By midnight of that date it was generally believed, all over the Union, that Lincoln and Johnson were overwhelmingly elected, and that the Life as well as Freedom of the Nation had thus been saved by the People.

Late that very night, President Lincoln was serenaded by a Pennsylvania political club, and, in responding to the compliment, modestly said:

"I earnestly believe that the consequences of this day's work (if it be as you assure, and as now seems probable) will be to the lasting advantage, if not to the very salvation, of the Country. I cannot at this hour say what has been the result of the election. But whatever it may be, I have no desire to modify this opinion, that all who have labored to-day in behalf of the Union organization have wrought for the best interests of their Country and the World, not only for the present but for all future ages.

"I am thankful to God," continued he, "for this approval of the People; but, while deeply gratified for this mark of their confidence in me, if I know my heart, my gratitude is free from any taint of personal triumph. I do not impugn the motives of any one opposed to me. It is no pleasure to me to triumph over any one; but I give thanks to the Almighty for this evidence of the People's resolution to stand by Free Government and the rights of Humanity."

On the 10th of November, in response to another serenade given at the White House, in the presence of an immense and jubilantly enthusiastic gathering of Union men, by the Republican clubs of the District of Columbia, Mr. Lincoln said:

"It has long been a grave question whether any Government, not too strong for the Liberties of its People, can be strong enough to maintain its existence in great emergencies. On this point the present Rebellion. has brought our Republic to a severe test, and a Presidential election, occurring in regular course during the Rebellion, has added not a little to the strain. * * * But the election, along with its incidental and undesired strife, has done good, too. It has demonstrated that a People's Government can sustain a National election in the midst of a great Civil War, until now it has not been known to the World that this was a possibility. It shows, also, how sound and how strong we still are.

"But," said he, "the Rebellion continues; and now that the election is over, may not all having a common interest reunite in a common effort to save our common Country?

"For my own part," continued he—as the cheering, elicited by this forcible appeal, ceased—"I have striven, and shall strive, to avoid placing any obstacle in the way. So long as I have been here I have not willingly planted a thorn in any man's bosom. While I am deeply sensible to the high compliment of a reelection, and duly grateful, as I trust, to Almighty God for having directed my countrymen to a right conclusion, as I think, for their own good, it adds nothing to my satisfaction that any other man may be disappointed or pained by the result."

And, as the renewed cheering evoked by this kindly, Christian utterance died away again, he impressively added: "May I ask those who have not differed with me, to join with me in this same spirit, towards those who have?"

So, too, on the 17th of November, in his response to the complimentary address of a delegation of Union men from Maryland.

[W. H. Purnell, Esq., in behalf of the Committee, delivered an address, in which he said they rejoiced that the People, by such an overwhelming and unprecedented majority, had again reelected Mr. Lincoln to the Presidency and endorsed his course—elevating him to the proudest and most honorable position on Earth. They felt under deep obligation to him because he had appreciated their condition as a Slave-State. It was not too much to say that by the exercise of rare discretion on his part, Maryland to-day occupies her position in favor of Freedom. Slavery has been abolished therefrom by the Sovereign Decree of the People. With deep and lasting gratitude they desired that his Administration, as it had been approved in the past, might also be successful in the future, and result in the Restoration of the Union, with Freedom as its immutable basis. They trusted that, on retiring from his high and honorable position, the universal verdict might be that he deserved well of mankind, and that favoring Heaven might 'Crown his days with loving kindness and tender mercies.']

The same kindly anxiety to soften and dispel the feeling of bitterness that had been engendered in the malignant bosoms of the Copperhead-Democracy by their defeat, was apparent when he said with emphasis and feeling:

"I have said before, and now repeat, that I indulge in no feeling of triumph over any man who has thought or acted differently from myself. I have no such feeling toward any living man;" and again, after complimenting Maryland for doing "more than double her share" in the elections, in that she had not only carried the Republican ticket, but also the Free Constitution, he added: "Those who have differed with us and opposed us will yet see that the result of the Presidential election is better for their own good than if they had been successful."

The victory of the Union-Republican Party at this election was an amazing one, and in the words of General Grant's dispatch of congratulation to the President, the fact of its "having passed off quietly" was, in itself, "a victory worth more to the Country than a battle won,"—for the Copperheads had left no stone unturned in their efforts to create the utmost possible rancor, in the minds of their partisans, against the Administration and its Party.

Of twenty-five States voting, Lincoln and Johnson had carried the electoral votes of twenty-two of them, viz.: Maine, New Hampshire, Massachusetts, Rhode Island, Connecticut, Vermont, New York, Pennsylvania, Maryland, Ohio, Indiana, Illinois, Missouri, Michigan, Iowa, Wisconsin, Minnesota, California, Oregon, Kansas, West Virginia, and Nevada; while McClellan and Pendleton had carried the twenty-one electoral votes of the remaining three, viz.: New Jersey, Delaware, and Kentucky—the popular vote reaching the enormous number of 2,216,067 for Lincoln, to 1,808,725 for McClellan—making Lincoln's popular majority 407,342, and his electoral majority 191!

But if the figures upon the Presidential candidacy were so gratifying and surprising to all who held the cause of Union above all others, no less gratifying and surprising were those of the Congressional elections, which indicated an entire revulsion of popular feeling on the subject of the Administration's policy. For, while in the current Congress (the 38th), there were only 106 Republican-Union to 77 Democratic Representatives, in that for which the elections had just been held, (the 39th), there would be 143 Republican-Union to 41 Democratic Representatives.

It was at once seen, therefore, that, should the existing House of Representatives fail to adopt the Thirteenth Amendment to the Constitution, there would be much more than the requisite two-thirds majority for such a Measure in both Houses of the succeeding Congress;

and moreover that in the event of its failure at the coming Session, it was more than probable that President Lincoln would consider himself justified in calling an Extra Session of the Thirty-ninth Congress for the especial purpose of taking such action. So far then, as the prospects of the Thirteenth Amendment were concerned, they looked decidedly more encouraging.